On Death: Helping Children
Understand and Cope

Sara Smilansky

On Death

Helping Children Understand and Cope

PETER LANG
New York · Berne · Frankfurt am Main · Paris

Library of Congress Cataloging-in-Publication Data

Smilansky, Sara.
On Death.
    Bibliography: p.
    1. Thanatology.   2. Children and death.   3. Death.
I. Title.
HQ1073.S55   1987   155.9'37   87-3922
ISBN 0-8204-0525-6

CIP-Kurztitelaufnahme der Deutschen Bibliothek

Smilansky, Sara:

On death: helping children understand and cope /
Sara Smilansky.– New York; Berne; Frankfurt am Main;
Paris: Lang, 1987.
ISBN 0-8204-0525-6

Printed by Weihert-Druck GmbH, Darmstadt (West Germany)

In Memory of my Mother-in-Law
Dr. Braha Smilansky

TABLE OF CONTENTS

ACKNOWLEDGEMENTS

This book is based on a number of research projects, experiments and workshops conducted by the author, each including one or more of the following sample populations:

1. Orphans* aged 4-12: children who lost their father or mother by death (N = 476).
2. Children aged 4 - 12, Non-orphans, control group (N = 472).
3. Kindergarten and elementary school teachers (N = 220).
4. Social workers, psychologists and counselors (N = 110).
5. Parents from different socio-economic groups
6. Adults who lost their father or mother in childhood (N = 72).

Without their cooperation the author would not have the basic data for this book.

My thanks to the staff of the Department of Casualties of the Israeli Air Force, who have, since 1970, allowed me to participate as a volunteer in their efforts to aid widows and orphans.

Thanks to the teachers, principals, special education staff, parents and children who allowed me to learn form them.

Thanks to the students of the Psychology Department and the School of Education of Tel Aviv University for all they have taught me.

I wish to thank T. Weisman, L. Haan, H. Amit, T. Man and E. Pardes for their help in the various stages of my study on children's conceptualization of death.

Although I am not a poet, I felt the need to express some of my ideas in the form of verse. My thanks to R. Tsadka and to M. Hituv for their literary editing of the poems.

I wish to thank the teachers, the resource staff and the parents who read the manuscript and whose comments helped me to adapt this book to their needs.

---

*   In this book, the word *orphan* refers to a child who lost his father *or* mother by death.

SPECIAL ACKNOWLEDGEMENTS

I wish to express my gratitude to the Board of Jewish Education of Greater Washington, D.C., for having initiated steps to translate my book into English and for offering Editorial Help and advice to facilitate effective implementation of the material in American schools.

I am also thankful to the United Jewish Endowment Fund of the United Appeal Federation of Greater Washington, D.C., for the grant of money which funded the translation.

In particular, I wish to thank Miriam Feinberg of the Board of Jewish Education, Dr. Uzi Ben Ami of the Jewish Social Service Agency, and Alice Lazar of the Prince George's County, Maryland Public School System, who offered editorial advice and to the following members of the review committee: Lynn Arons and Edith Lowy of the Charles E. Smith Jewish Day School of Greater Washington, D.C., Dorothy Bernstein of the Jewish Social Service Agency of Greater Washington, D.C. and Rena Rotenberg of the Board of Jewish Education of Greater Baltimore, Maryland.

I wish to thank Shoshana Rothschild for the translation of the book into English.

INTRODUCTION

In introducing this book I would like to stress once more the importance of the help rendered by the school to the bereaved pupil and to his family. Helping a bereaved child at a time of crisis may appear to be the task of his family or of a professional in the field of mental care. This book, however, is based on the approach which views the school and the teacher as a natural support system for the child in one of the most difficult crises of his life.

The teacher is a figure significant to the child and close to him, yet not a member of his family. This fact endows him with the neutrality and stability that a person must have in order to be able to give support in a time of crisis. Moreover, the teacher is easily accessible both to the child and to his family, and he/she does not carry the daunting stigma of professionals in the field of mental health. The teacher can react quickly and on the spot, thereby preventing various undesirable developments.

From my own personal experience, and from the experience of fellow-psychologists working in schools, I am convinced that despite the discomfort, the anxiety and the insecurity often aroused by contact with grief, many teachers are willing to deal with the problem and offer their support when needed. There are some teachers who are daunted by the problem and unwilling to take any interventive action. Others have acted with hesitation because they were unaware of the child's needs and did not know how to react appropriately. I have found that despite the defensive reaction that is typical of most people who come in contact with bereavement, particularly the bereaved child, people are able and willing to help after they are better informed on the subject. Herein lies the important contribution of this book.

In this book Professor Smilansky has gathered a wealth of material which provides the teacher with detailed information on the development of the concept of death in children and on the needs of the mourning child. She has provided guidelines on dealing with the mourning child and with his family. Professor Smilansky presents the reader with a comprehensive view of the subject based on research conducted in Israel and on data from many studies in the U.S.A. and other countries. She presents typical questions asked by both teachers and children, as well as answers to the questions. The questions have been gathered from interviews of the author with individual teachers, teacher-groups and with bereaved families. The answers are based on the findings of the author's research and on findings of numerous other studies, as well as on her clinical experience in working with people in crisis.

Death is an inseparable part of life and in the course of his/her work the teacher encounters children in whose family there has been a tragedy. It is therefore particularly important that teachers acquire the information imparted by this book, and not only when it is necessitated by an actual case of death.

It is clear to me that a teacher who is equipped with this information will be better able to help the bereaved pupil and his family, and will feel more confident of his task in a time of crisis. The teacher who knows more about the subject and who understands it better will be more willing to initiate a closer contact with a child undergoing a crisis. This relationship will then broaden to include the other children in the class, who also need help and support at a time when they are feeling uncertain and confused as a result of their classmate's tragedy. This teacher will also be able to motivate and organize the class to offer support to the orphaned child. Thus the teacher's power to help is enhanced and the bereaved child's chances of readjustment are increased.

Dr. Amiram Raviv
Chief Psychologist
Psychological Counseling Service
Ministry of Education and Culture
Israel.

PREFACE

The American Reviewing Committee

In June of 1984, Prof. Sara Smilansky met with a group of teachers, educators, psychologists and rabbis from the Greater Washington area at the Board of Jewish Education of Greater Washington. At that meeting, Prof. Smilansky described her research with parents, spouses and children of Israeli Air Force members who were killed during Israel's Six-Day-War. In her research she gathered new information on children's abilities to learn concepts of death. Subsequently, she developed a series of educational techniques designed to help school personnel and parents teach death concepts to young children in anticipation of inevitable experience with death during their lives. Her research findings have been included in the book *Dealing with Death — Children Aged 3-12*. The book has proven very successful in helping to teach death concepts to Israeli children.

While the group with which Prof. Smilansky met at the Board of Jewish Education was impressed with the importance of her work, there were two concerns: a) the book was available only in Hebrew and b) it was mainly relevant to Israeli society and therefore mainly to Israeli children. It was acknowledged that impressive though the work is, it would be widely appropriate for use in the United States only if it was translated into English and adapted for use with American children. With this in mind the following events occurred:

The Early Childhood Department of the Board of Jewish Education of Greater Washington successfully secured a grant from the Washington, D.C. area United Jewish Endowment Fund and from Mr. Harold Nussbaum of Washington, D.C. for the purpose of funding the translation of Prof. Smilansky's work. Shoshana Rothschild was engaged to translate the book into English.

Upon completion of the translation, a reviewing committee conferred on the appropriateness and usefulness of the work. Group members were Dr. Uzi Ben Ami, psychologist and Dorothy Bernstein, social worker of the Jewish Social Service Agency, Rockville, Maryland, Lynn Arons, school counselor and Edith Lowy, teacher

16

of the Charles E. Smith Jewish Day School, Rockville, MD, Alice Lazar, school psychologist, Prince Georges County Public Schools, Maryland, Rena Rotenberg, Early Childhood Educator, Board of Jewish Education, Baltimore, Maryland, and Miriam Feinberg, Early Childhood Educator, Board of Jewish Education of Greater Washington, D.C. At the group's direction, Dr. Ben Ami, Mrs. Lazar and Mrs. Feinberg edited the manuscript with the goal in mind of adapting the material to American society.

The reviewing committee members have expressed the essential need for children to understand death concepts if they are to deal effectively with life. It is appropriate for parents and school personnel to be concerned with this issue along with all other issues affecting the lives of children as they develop. In its present form, Prof. Smilansky's book should be considered an appropriate guide and highly desirable for use in the U.S.A. by parents and school personnel who deal with children aged 4-12.

17

Part One:

THE DEVELOPMENT OF THE CONCEPT OF DEATH AMONG CHILDREN

Chapter 1. Children's Confrontation with Death

Death is a natural and inevitable phenomenon. It is inherent in life because it is the inescapable end of all life: flowers wilt, animals and humans die. Moreover, death is a phenomenon over which we have no control. Although we have discovered many of nature's secrets, we do not have a solution for the mystery of death. It is no wonder, then, that man, feeling completely helpless when he confronts death, experiences severe anxiety connected with this phenomenon, which he tries to deal with in various ways.

One of the causes of the great difficulty experienced by modern man in dealing with death is the fact that the natural initial reaction of denial has become a generally accepted social norm. There is a noticeable tendency to avoid talking about death, a kind of social taboo reminiscent of the taboo against speaking of sex, prevalent in the last century. It seems that, today, parents find it easier to speak to their children about the source of life than about its termination.

It must be stressed that difficulty in dealing with death is present in all instances of death, even when we do not know the deceased personally. When we hear of anonymous accident-casualties or of the death of a well-known public figure, we are being confronted with death. Our reaction might be a feeling of sorrow and sympathy or we might try to ignore the death.

In Israel the widespread confrontation with death is even more apparent. The cohesiveness of Israeli society and the realization that though spared today, we may be the one stricken the following day, give rise to a feeling of a common fate and to mourning in social frameworks, wider than those of the immediate family. The general identification of the people in the country with our war casualties serves as a good illustration of this. The confrontation with death, however, is obviously more difficult when one loses someone near and dear to him. In such cases the mourner struggling with his pain generally finds himself in the company of people just as disoriented and helpless as himself. The anxiety aroused by the encounter with death is severe. Feelings of anxiety and helplessness, which are caused by the general social taboo on dealing with the subject of death prevalent in a secular society, are most extremely felt during the period of mourning. A study of the process and customs of mourning which was conducted in Britain (1981) revealed a tendency to minimize mourning as much as possible. There are very few customs or other behavior patterns associated with mourning. This points to a general lack of understanding of the needs of the mourner. It seems that in our society, too, expression of feelings is perceived as irrational surrender to immature impulses, rather than being understood as an essential expression of a psychological need. People who attend funerals or call on the bereaved family during the Shiv'a (the seven days of mourning customary among Jews) behave in a very reserved manner and refrain from mentioning the deceased. The bereaved family is directly or indirectly encouraged to 'overcome' its grief and return to 'a normal life' as soon as possible.

In view of the difficulty faced by adults in dealing with death, it is no wonder that children, who are naturally curious about the mysteries of life, encounter a curtain of denial, disregard and evasion, and even false explanations, when they ask questions. Children show great curiosity on the subject of death and it is one of the important subjects which continue to concern them. A young child tends to endow inanimate objects (such as toys), plants and animals with human properties. A young child will talk to a toy dog and 'feed' it, will treat a cat like a baby, and so on. When the child loses such an object, he first faces the phenomenon of absolute cessation of things that were dear to him and which were a part of the routine of his life. Later on, the child experiences reactions of mourning when a flower which he nurtured dies or when his dog is run over. In addition to such personal encounters with death, chance encounters such as observing dead birds and animals or killing insects contribute to the child's preoccupation with death. Naturally, cases of death in the child's immediate family, such as the death of a grandparent, sibling or parent, deepen the child's contemplation of the phenomenon of death.

In effect, we can distinguish three levels of a child's involvement with death:

1. Preoccupation with the subject of death on the part of children who are not personally affected. This preoccupation, which involves thinking about death, asking questions about it, and wondering about its meaning, is reinforced by impersonal everyday occurrences in the child's life such as hearing a memorial service, encountering a dead bird, or seeing about death on T.V.

2. Involvement with the subject of death as a result of a personal encounter with death, albeit not a direct encounter; the death of a friend's father or of a neighbor, for instance. In this case, in addition to thinking and wondering about death, the child sometimes experiences strong emotions, stemming from his personal acquaintance with the deceased and from confusion about how to behave with the mourners.

3. Being directly and personally affected by death, as in the case of the loss of a close member of the child's family or a close friend.

Although the child, just like an adult, experiences an emotional reaction to death and has to deal with it in one way or another, adults tend to ignore this fact rather than trying to help the child to deal with it. Not only are the child's questions about death usually left unanswered, but his emotional need to mourn the loss of people close to him, in his own way, is not recognised. Such behavior on the part of adults is common not only among parents but also among professional people – teachers, counselors, psychologists, social workers, etc. – whose profession provides them with the opportunity and, indeed, charges them with the responsibility of helping the child in his encounter with death.

When these adults are asked to explain their behavior, they usually cite the child's tender age. Some contend that a very young child is unable to deal with a 'heavy' and painful subject such as death and therefore must be prevented from concerning himself with it, 'to save him pain' so that his mental health is not impaired. Others claim that at such a young age the child is incapable of understanding a subject as complex as death. The behavior of adults, however, often reflects a sincere and genuine bewilderment. Even those who think that a child should be helped to deal with death are often afraid to act because they do not know how to act. Many teachers, counselors, doctors, nurses, say they were not trained to deal with such a subject and have no idea of how to approach it, although they recognize the child's need for guidance in dealing with death.

This book deals with the ways in which children can be helped to deal with death.

Chapter 2: The Significance of Preventive aid to Children on the Subject of Death

A child may approach the phenomenon of death from two different points of reference, the first being the *cognitive approach*. What is death? What is the connection between life and death? Does a dead person lose the properties of life? Will he ever return to life? The second point of reference is the *emotional approach*. What do we feel when someone close to us dies? What do we feel when a person is being buried? What do we feel when a dog dies? Who is to blame for death?

The child needs help from adults in his efforts to deal with death on both the cognitive and the emotional levels. Adults must help the child to understand death correctly, depending on his level of understanding. They must help him to feel the implications of death in a natural manner. Both of these aspects are important and complement each other.

When such assistance is offered the child only in cases when someone close to him and on whom he is dependent has died, its effectiveness is doubtful even when the person offering assistance sincerely wishes to help. In such cases strong emotions cloud the understanding, and the severe pain of mourning which the child is experiencing prevents him from correctly understanding what has happened. It is precisely those cases of misfortune in which the child is not personally close to the deceased which can be more effectively employed for purposes of preventive aid in dealing with the problem of death. Here the child is less emotionally involved.

Adults frequently ignore occurrences of death (of an animal or of a public personage) or try to hide them from children ("Turn off the T.V. This is not something a child ought to hear" or when finding a dead bird "Let's walk a different way. There is something here that is not a very pretty sight"). Such chance opportunities should be used to prepare the child for a more serious and personal confrontation with death.

In such 'general' cases, or whenever a child shows curiosity about the phenomenon of death, he should receive a calm, relaxed explanation of what death means. On this occasion his/her ability to understand will be greater, since he/she is not deeply and personally involved.

More emotionally neutral opportunities can also serve to prepare the child emotionally, since they give him a chance to hear people voicing their feelings about death and to see people expressing grief, along with the anxiety, fear and frustration accompanying grief. The child will accept all this as natural. When he/she is later confronted by a death that is closer to him/her personally (for a child, the death of a friend's father may be close enough), he/she will not try to repress his/her feelings and will not hesitate to express them openly.

Cognitive and emotional preparation is very like immunization of the body against an illness. When the body is immunized, it is given a light attack of the illness, which immunizes it against a more severe attack in the future. The child who experiences 'a light dose' of mourning will be prepared to deal more effectively with 'the more severe' cases of personal misfortune. It must be stressed that I am not claiming that the child will be protected from pain and grief in case of the death of someone close to him. I am maintaining only that in such cases the child will find it easier to deal with death if he has had such preparation, most likely emerging from his encounter with death with fewer frustrations and with a better understanding of the phenomenon of death. Such preparation before a personal misfortune strikes is an experience which is helpful not only to the child but also to the adult trying to help him. The adult finds it easier in this situation to think of what is good for the child, to explain, to comfort and to help him/her, than in a situation when they are mourning the loss of someone near and dear to them both.

Chapter 3: The Place of the Teacher in Rendering Preventive Aid

It may be asked whether the teacher's role entails dealing with the subject of death in the classroom, as a means of preventive aid to prepare the child for an acute encounter with death in the future. Mitchell (1969), maintains that it is the role of the teacher to provide the child with opportunities for developing ways which will lead him to a better adult life by developing the ability to deal effectively with situations which he is likely to encounter. She emphasizes that developing this ability depends on several factors related to the teacher:

1. The relationship between the teacher and the child, and the degree of self-confidence and self-esteem which the teacher imparts to the child by means of this relationship.

2. The extent to which the teacher succeeds in creating a supportive and accepting atmosphere.

3. The extent to which the teacher encourages the child's curiosity and his wish to discover and understand things, and the extent to which the teacher helps the child to apply and act on the things he has discovered.

Grollman, (1976), emphasizes the importance of the teacher as a model of emulation in the development of his pupils. In his opinion, an example of behavior is more effective and has a more forceful influence on pupils than verbal instructions. Brown, (1975), stresses the importance of the teacher as a model of emulation in furthering his pupil's process of socialization. The pupil's sense of right and wrong, his opinions, his values, his manner of solving problems, and his social behavior are influenced by the example of the teacher. The teacher should exploit his/her role as a model of emulation and the special elements of the pupil-teacher relationship for the purpose of developing in the pupils a sensitivity for the needs of the mourner.

It must be remembered that a child has a great deal of curiosity concerning death. Death is one of the important subjects with which he concerns himself throughout his development and which accompany him into adulthood. Even when the child is not personally affected, as in the case of the death of a close relative, his emotional involvement is inevitable and is generally accompanied by fears and anxieties about what might happen to him or to his loved ones. A teacher must not, therefore, treat death as a subject not to be mentioned, thinking that open discussion of the subject might create problems where none exist. Children are concerned with and bothered by death. It is the teacher's task to acknowledge the child's fears and help him to understand the concept of death and its various elements in a realistic manner.

Chapter 4: The Central Aspects in the the Concept of Death

On the basis of my clinical experience working with orphaned* children and analysis of the process of mourning and readjustment of the orphan, as well as on the basis of existing theories and of our empirical studies previously conducted on the subject, (Smilansky 1976; 77; 80; 81), we concluded that the concept of death includes five principal aspects. A proper understanding of these aspects is a precondition for the child's unencumbered passage through the process of mourning and for his subsequent readjustment. These five aspects are: the irreversibility of death, the finality of death, the causality of death, the inevitability of death, and old age.

a) The Irreversibility of Death

Understanding this concept involves understanding that death is an irreversible phenomenon, a state from which there is no return or recovery. The deceased can never return to be a living person, no matter how much we wish it. Understanding this concept also involves giving up the deceased as a living person forever, and recognizing the impossibility of changing the course of biological life and returning to a previous state. It is of vital significance in the first stage of the mourning process. The mourning child may refuse to accept the fact – emotionally as well as intellectually – that his father (or mother, brother, or grandfather) will not return to him. He may try therefore, to recall the deceased by wishing (magical thinking) and by clinging to customs associated with the returning of the deceased (keeping the door open, waiting for him outside, etc.). Only when the child is convinced that the deceased isn't coming back, and when he/she understands that the dead will never return as living persons, can he/she begin the second stage of mourning. This involves working through the feelings associated with parting with a loved one forever.

---

* In this book, the word *orphan* refers to a child who lost his father *or* mother by death.

Cognitive acceptance of the irreversibility of death is the first condition for preparing the child to accept his feelings about the fact of everlasting separation. Understanding the irreversibility of death is important for the child's readjustment as well. Without first accepting the fact that his/her father is gone forever, the child cannot reorganize his life. Readjustment means reorganization of personal frames of reference as well as of social relationships and patterns of life. Such reorganization must be based on recognition of the need for reorganization, since the change that has taken place is permanent. Understanding the concept of the irreversibility of death is, therefore, an essential condition for the mourning process and for the readjustment of the child.

b) The Finality of Death

Understanding this concept involves perceiving the state of death as the converse of the state of living, a state in which all functions of life (metabolic functions, motion, sensation, and consciousness) cease. A child who understands the concept of the finality of death gradually accepts the fact that the deceased is no longer alive in any sense and is not a living person. Understanding the finality of death helps the child to accept the fact of a death. Afertwards, it helps the child to bear his grief, since he understands that the deceased is in no way suffering. He does not feel cold, hunger or pain from the wound or illness from which he died. Once the child is freed from the need to worry about his deceased parent, he can concentrate on his own grief, and on his longing for the deceased. This process opens the way for the process of mourning and the child's subsequent readjustment.

The proper understanding of the finality of death is important during the bereavement and readjustment phase, since such perception helps the child to understand that the deceased no longer exists as a living person and that in death he is entirely different from what he was when alive. The child can thus learn that he need not continue to relate to the dead person in the same way he related to him when he was alive. He is thereby free to form new emotional attachments, even with a new parent. He is able to accept the fact that such a new attachment does not constitute a betrayal of the dead parent. Since the parent is no longer 'a person', and he cannot feel hunger, cold or pain, the child need not worry about him.

c) The Causality of Death

The concept of causality of death relates to the physical-biological factors that led to the death. The child must first of all understand the concept of causality of death in general. He must then know the specific causes which led to the death of the loved one. This knowledge can in some measure ease the pain of the child, who, like any other mourner, wonders about the cause of the death of his loved one and is troubled by feelings of guilt related to the cause of the death.

Knowing the actual cause of death will help the bereaved child in the second stage of mourning. During this stage the child frequently experiences feelings of anger against the deceased parent, as well as feelings of self-blame and blame of those around him and of the deceased himself. Cognitive understanding is no insurance against feelings of guilt. But together with the proper emotional working through of the child's feelings, it gives the child a good chance for resolution of his mourning and for readjustment.

The proper perception of the causality of death and release from feelings of guilt are, as has been shown, helpful in the readjustment of the child. As long as the child is preoccupied by the problem of the causes of death and troubled by feelings of guilt, which tie him to the past, it is impossible for him to establish a new set of behavior patterns. It is likewise impossible for him to establish a new frame of reference to others. Guilt is the cornerstone of neurosis. It is an important factor in delaying the healthy emotional development of the child. This is even more emphatically true when the guilt feelings are related to the trauma of the loss of a father, mother, or sibling.

The bereaved child can be aided by being helped to understand the various causes of death reationally, and by receiving suitable emotional aid. This enables him to mourn and to readjust, helped by the knowledge that neither he/she, nor the people close to him are to blame for the death.

d) *The Inevitability of Death*

The concept of inevitability of death involves treating death as a natural phenomenon which is inherently inevitable. Understanding death's inevitability involves perceiving death as a universal phenomenon from which no living thing can escape. The proper conceptualization of the inevitability of death helps the child in the last stage of mourning. In this stage he/she adjusts to the new reality and reorganizes his/her personality. Understanding the inevitability of death also indirectly helps the child to understand the causality of death. If a child understands that death is universal, and that if a person doesn't die of one cause, he will eventually die of another, he will more readily grasp the real cause of the death. Moreover, this understanding will reduce guilt. The child will understand that death, being universal, comes to all people, and that it is unlikely that the child's anger, for instance, was the cause of his father's death.

Understanding the inevitability of death also provides the orphaned child with a measure of comfort. The orphan feels alone, different from other children, singled out for misfortune. Orphans ask such questions as, "Why was it that only my father was killed in the war (or accident, or disease), while all the other fathers returned home?". If the child grasps that every child's father must eventually die, he/she will find it somewhat easier, by the end of the period of mourning, to accept the inevitable, knowing that the grief he/she has known is, at some time or other, experienced by all people.

e) *Old Age*

The four concepts described above reflect the connection between cognitive understanding and the emotional processes of mourning and readjustment. An additional concept, old age, was included in our study, conducted among kindergarten and elementary school children. The concept of old age is related to an understanding of death but not to the process of mourning. Understanding old age involves understanding the biological sequence of life: birth, growth, aging and death. The concept of old age is related to the concepts of inevitability and causality. Based on a pilot study, I found that in examining the concept of death it was necessary to include a specific question relating to old age. It appears that children sometimes understand the concepts of causality and inevitability as they apply to death but they do not understand them as they apply to old age. A child may say that old age is the cause of death, but he may not understand that all people age. He may understand that all people age but not that all people die. For purposes of diagnosis for intervention, the first four concepts are of special significance. For purposes of studying a child's or a group of children's conceptualization of death and obtaining a complete picture, the concept of old age should be included. See our Guestionnaire for Examination of Human and animal Death Conceptualization of children Aged 4-12 and its Psychometric Characteristics, page 195.

Chapter 5: Development of the Concepts of Death —
A Survey of the Literature

In order to help a child effectively in dealing with death it is not enough for the adult to understand that the child has a need to deal with the subject or to mourn the loss of someone dear to him. While recognition of such needs in a child is a vital condition for helping him this is not sufficient.

Another vital condition for helping the child is knowing the development of a child's understanding of the concept of death. A teacher with the best of intentions will find it difficult to help a child to deal with death or to discover the serious problems that are troubling him, if in her explanations she uses concepts which the child does not understand. This section deals with the development in children of the conceptualization of death. We shall try to gain an understanding of this development by reviewing the findings of studies conducted in the U.S.A. and in other countries.

Mitchell, (1969), claims that by observing animal and plant life, the child discovers the fact that the world is not constant and that changes take place in every organism. This awareness of the concept of change in living things leads the child to the threshold of understanding death. Anthony, (1971), on the other hand, claims that it is the child's awareness of himself, rather than his observation of plant and animal life, that leads him to understand the concept of death. The transition from sleep to waking and vice versa is the first experience that leads a child to awareness of different states of being. In Anthony's opinion, the fear of going to bed, among children aged one and two, is proof of the parallel that children draw between sleeping and ceasing to be, and between being awake and being. Moriatry, (1976), finds support of this opinion in games that young children play. He holds that children's frequent games of hide-and-seek, and the pleasure a baby shows in 'finding' his mother after she has hidden from him, support the assumption that young children possess a partial understanding of different states of being.

Kastenbaum, (1967), notes that a baby's experience of short and long periods of separation from those close to him serves as the basis for later conceptualization of death. In the first few years of his life a child exhibits a certain interest in the processes of life and its termination. He experiences various 'death-like' phenomena. Nevertheless, all researchers agree that a child does not form a rudimentary definable perception of death before the age of three or four. According to Kastenbaum the main reason for this is that until this age a child does not yet possess the cognitive tools necessary for understanding the concepts connected with death.

The second stage of perception of the concept of death occurs at about the age of four or five. At this stage the child begins to understand, though only partially, the sub-concepts of death. In her study, Nagy, (1965), found that children at this age perceive death as an aspect of life. For a child of this age, to die means to live in a different state. Death is not perceived as a final and unchangeable state, but rather as a temporary alternative to life, similar to sleep.

The third stage in the development of the child's concept of death occurs between the ages of five and nine. At this stage, the child understands that death is final and inevitable. Nevertheless, he/she still finds it difficult to accept the possibility of his/her own death. Kastenbaum (1967), found that the majority of six and seven-year-olds doubt that their parents will die someday or that they themselves will die. That is to say, although the child recognizes the finality of death and he/she accepts the fact that death is a state in which all functions of life cease, he/she still does not recognize the inevitability of death and its universality. According to Kastenbaum this denial of personal death may stem from the child's extreme emotional vulnerability at this age. A complete recognition of death is delayed to a later time, when the child will possess the emotional means for coping with the personal-emotional aspects of death.

Nagy, (1959), found that at this age a childish way of thinking is prevalent, which commonly endows the dead with certain properties of life (personifying death). Death is described by children aged five to nine as a man or as a skeleton. At the same time, they understand that life and death are opposite concepts. Only after the age of nine, in the fourth and final stage, is death perceived by the child as a universal phenomenon that follows certain laws which are not in our power to control. Nagy claims that when a child understands that death is an internal process, he/she understands its universal nature and its inevitability. Other researchers, such as Anthony, (1971), Piaget, (1955), and Kastenbaum, (1972), attribute the beginnings of a mature perception of death to an older age — between ten and eleven. They argue that this is the approximate age at which the child is equipped with the intellectual skills necessary for a logical understanding of life and death. According to Piaget, maturation of such concepts as time, distance, quantity and causality provides the child with a frame of reference within which he is able to place the concept of death.

There are differences among different researchers in the ages at which they set the beginning and the end of each stage in the development of the child's conceptualization of death as well as the way in which they explain each stage. There is nevertheless one distinctive feature common to most researchers. They all see the four stages in the development of the child's conceptualization of death as part of the process of cognitive maturation of the child. The further along the child is in his development of such cognitive tools as understanding the concepts of time, causality, and inevitability as they relate to death, the more complete will be his general understanding of the concept of death. However, even the most ardent disciples of the stage theorists, do not doubt the fact that there are other factors which affect the development of the child's conceptualization of death. The principal factor suggested by Kastenbaum and Mitchell is the influence of the society and the environment in which the child lives. The child's environment may, in various ways, help him to gain a better understanding of the concept of death. One such way, discussed in Alexander and Alexander's (1965) study of attitudes to death among children with a religious background, is by letting the child participate in the customs and ceremonies of mourning. Mitchell considers experience of the death of animals, accompanied by a suitable explanation, as a factor which speeds conceptualization of death.

Anna Freud, (1953), found that children who were living in London during World War II grasped certain aspects of death at the age of two or three. They particularly understood the causality and irreversibility of death. Furman, (1964), emphasizes mainly the

34

suitable explanation as a factor which helps the child to gain a better understanding of death. He maintains that it is possible to explain death to very young children, two and three-year-olds. Barnes, (1964), has shown that with the help of professional counseling young children succeeded in understanding death. They therefore experience a normal mourning process.

Smilansky & Knaani, (1975), illustrated some of the various spheres in which the environment (in this case, the Israeli environment) can affect children's conceptualization of death. They compared children of pilots and air-crews living on an airforce base with children living in an ordinary city environment, in their conceptualization of death. Smilansky & Knaani asumed that the environment at the airbase was different from the environment in the city in variables relevant to a child's conceptualization of death. For example, beginning with the first months of their lives, children living on an airbase experience separation of a nature described by several researchers as critical in the conceptualization of death. These children are also aware of the danger of death which their fathers face whenever they go out on a mission. They sense the anxiety of their mothers while waiting for their husbands' return, and they are touched by the experience of the death of someone close. The families living on a base form a closely-knit and intimate community. When there is a death in one family, all the other families share the grief of and identify with the stricken family. This fact is very significant for children. Awareness among airbase children of death in their immediate surroundings is much greater than among city children, who live within the sphere of their family and who are less involved in the lives of non-family members. The Israeli study, in fact, showed that airbase children aged 4 - 5 are able to conceptualize death on a higher level than city children of the same age and the same level of intelligence. These findings support the claim of Mitchell (1969) and Kastenbaum (1972) that environmental experience advances a child's conceptualization of death.

Chapter 6: Development of the Concepts of Death among Israeli Children — Research Findings

In order to equip the teacher with tools which will enable him/ her to guide the children of his/her class towards understanding the concept of death, we needed first to establish at what age and on what level Israeli children conceptualize death.

Israeli society constitutes a unique environment in which death is a constant and frequent occurrence, which is often experienced and talked about, mainly due to our security situation. The question arises whether Israeli children conceptualize death at an earlier age and on a higher level than do children of other countries?

Our study of the correlation of the Israeli child's level of conceptualizing death to other factors shows that age is the dominant factor affecting conceptualization of death. That is, the older the child, the more advanced the level of his conceptualization of death. The factor which is next in importance is the child's intelligence. There is a significant correlation between a child's intelligence and his understanding the concepts of death. A third factor which affects conceptualization of death among Israeli children is the parents' level of education. The higher the level of the parents' education, the better and earlier the child's conceptualization of death. See the graphs on pages 235-241.

Since our assumption that death is not a monolithic concept but is composed of five sub-concepts (irreversibility, finality, causality, inevitability, and old age), I attempted to examine the differences among children of various age groups in their understanding of these sub-concepts. Likewise I examined the differences among children of the same age group but with varying levels of intelligence and varying levels of parents' education. For this last purpose, the children were divided into two groups: Those whose parents had a high school or university education and children whose parents had not completed high school. The findings of this study and consideration of the ways in which the teacher can apply them follow.

The study consisted of interviews with elementary school children. The interviewer filled out two questionnaires — one relating to human death and the other to death of animals. The questionnaires included various questions about death* (what do people die of, do the dead see and hear, does everyone die, etc.), relating to each of the five aspects of death (described in section 4): Irreversibility, finality, causality, inevitability, and old age.

Each child received, on each aspect, a grade of between 0 and 3 points. Thus the total possible score on each questionnaire was 15, and the general inclusive grade on conceptualization of death (of humans and animals) ranged between 0 and 30 points.**

A. Development of the Concepts of Death Among Children From Pre-School Age to Fourth Grade.

The effect of age on a child's level of understanding of the concept of death expresses itself both in the widening of the range of his knowledge and in the maturity of his understanding. That is, an older child's perception of death includes a wider range of concepts and is characterized by a greater degree of maturity in the perception of each concept. The greatest progress in the understanding of the concept of death takes place between the ages of 4 and 5, between pre-kindergarten age and kindergarten age. (This progress is expressed in an advancement of 5 points in the general score.)

Between pre-kindergarten age and the second grade the child steadily progresses towards a better understanding of the concept of death. In the second grade there is a consolidation of this understanding, relating both to humans and animals. From this age on, there is little advancement in the understanding of death (the difference in the scores of second graders and fourth graders is a mere 1.5 points).

---

* See "Questionnaire for examination of human and animal death conceptualization of children" (page 195).
** See "Diagnostic summary record of an individual child's conceptualization of death" (page 203). Also see (page 235) for graphic presentation of findings.

B. Development of the Concept of Death. Comparison Between Two Groups of Children Based on the Level of their Parents' Education (see graph No 1, page 236)

The aim of the study was to establish the relationship between the level of the parents' education and the level of their children's conceptualization of death.

The study showed that in all age groups, from pre-schoolers to fourth graders, the children from the better educated families achieved higher marks in conceptualization of death. In addition, the study shows incomplete correspondence between the two groups of children in the rate of development of the concept of death: While both groups show the greatest progress (about 5 points) between pre-kindergarten and kindergarten age, the children from the better educated families show additional progress between kindergarten and second grade (2-3 points per year) and then consolidation between second and third grade, whereas the children from the poorly educated families show the second wave of progress between kindergarten and the third grade (2-3 points per year), and consolidation between third and fourth grade.

C. Development of the Concept of Irreversibility From Pre-Kindergarten Age to Fourth Grade (see graph No 2, Page 237)

The concept of death's irreversibility implies recognition of death as an irreversible phenomenon and a permanent relinquishment of the deceased as a living person. It signifies our inability to reverse the biological processes of life. In contrast to findings relating to all the other concepts which comprise the conceptualization of death, to be discussed in the following paragraphs, our study shows that children of all ages consistently exhibit a better understanding of the concept of irreversibility when applied to animal death than of the same concept when applied to human death.

The greatest progress in the understanding of the concept takes place between pre-kindergarten and kindergarten age. The entire process is marked by a transition from cognizance of the fact of

38

irreversibility accompanied by failure to grasp its significance to a fair understanding of its causes.

From first grade onward understanding of the concept of irreversibility becomes stabilized, and there are no significant differences between different age groups.

D. Development of the Concept Finality – From Pre-Kindergarten Age to the Fourth Grade (see graph No·3, page 238)

Understanding the concept of finality means understanding that death is the termination of all processes of life, visible or invisible. All the biological functions which characterize the living – such as use of the senses, the functioning of organs and consciousness – cease when the person dies. The deceased is no longer a person in any sense which characterizes the living.

The study shows that the level of conceptualization of the finality of death is similar for humans and animals.

Moreover, the study shows that a certain level of understanding of the concept exists as early as pre-kindergarten age. The average score (1.8-2.1) received by this age group indicates that a four-year-old child (pre-kindergarten age) understands the concept of finality of death, though his understanding is incomplete and he is not always able to name the causes of the facts which he refers to. The greatest progress in understanding the concept takes place between pre-kindergarten age and first grade.

When the child enters school he has a good understanding of the finality of death, and afterwards there is a moderate development towards a full understanding of the concept by the fourth grade (2.8 points out of 3).

E. Development of the Concept of Causality, from Pre-Kindergarten Age to Fourth Grade (see graph No 4, page 239)

The concept of causality involves understanding the causes leading to death, such as war, illness, old age, etc. The study shows that children understand the concept of causality better as it relates to humans than as it relates to animals, in almost all age groups.

There is no evident progress in understanding of the concept between pre-kindergarten age and kindergarten age. Both these age groups are characterized by a vague understanding of the causes of death. The greatest progress in understanding the concept occurs between kindergarten and first grade.

First grade is the age at which the concept of causality in general, as it relates to all phenomena in the child's world, reaches maturity. At this age the child tends to discontinue his magical thinking, which is characterized, among other things, by a belief in the power of thoughts and words to affect the course of his life and the lives of those around him, and becomes aware of the logical pattern of cause and effect in various occurrences. Accordingly, as shown by the findings, at this age there is great progress in the child's understanding of causality as related to death.

It should be noted, however, that even at the stage when the concept becomes consolidated, i.e., third and fourth grade, the children do not yet understand it fully and are not able to name all possible causes of death, including death from old age or as a result of certain occurrences.

F. Development of the Concept of Inevitability, from Pre-Kindergarten Age to Fourth Grade (see graph No 5, page 240)

The concept of the inevitability of death involves understanding that death, whatever its cause, is an inevitable occurrence.

The study shows that in all age groups children exhibit a better understanding of the inevitability of human death than they do of animal death. The study shows great progress in understanding the concept between pre-kindergarten age and second grade. While at pre-kindergarten age the child associates death only with certain people and certain events, but mostly not with himself, at school age he shows a certain awareness of old age as a cause of death, although he may not always understand the connection between the two, and although he may sometimes still exclude himself and his parents from the general rule.

These findings correspond with the studies of Kastenbaum (1967), who found that most 6-7-year-olds doubt that they or their parents will die. In second grade progress takes place towards the understanding that sooner or later everyone must die. This progress reaches its peak in fourth grade, a stage at which there is almost complete understanding of the concept.

G. Development of the Concept of Old Age, From Pre-Kindergarten Age to Fourth Grade (see graph No 6, page 241)

Understanding the concept of old age involves understanding the biological sequence of life, which impels all living things towards old age and, consequently, towards death.

The study reveals a large gap between the relatively good understanding of the concept of aging as it relates to humans and the inadequate understanding of the concept as it relates to animals. This gap narrows as the child gets older, but even in fourth grade it is still significant. It may be assumed that the cause for this difference in understanding lies in the fact that the process of aging is much more perceptible in humans than it is in animals. While a child can distinguish between an old person and a young one according to appearance, definition and attitude, he has no criteria for perceiving old age in animals. Therefore, understanding the aging process in animals requires a higher level of abstraction, which the child has not yet achieved by fourth grade.

The study shows that the greatest progress in understanding the concept of aging in humans occurs between pre-kindergarten age and kindergarten age. While four-year-olds show little understanding of the process of aging, five-year-olds are able to understand the process, though in many cases excluding themselves and those close to them from it. After the age of six the child steadily progresses towards a better understanding of the concept of old age. In third grade there is a consolidation and an almost complete understanding of the concept as it relates to humans, all humans, including the child's application of the aging process to himself.

H. Summation of our Most Notable Findings are:

1. The understanding of all 5 concepts increases with age, the most significant progress in understanding occurring between the ages of 4-6. After the third grade progress is much more gradual.
2. Conceptualization of human death is better than that of animal death. This is true of all age groups and of most of the concepts, with the exception of the concept of irreversibility, which children understand better as it relates to animals, and the concept of finality for which scores are about the same for human death and animal death.

The following section will deal with the concept of death in each age group separately.

Chapter 7: Development in Understanding of the Concept of Death Among Children of Various age Groups

A. Pre-kindergarten Age

The conceptualization of death among 4-5 year-olds is marked by a general immaturity, though death is by no means foreign to children of this age, nor, as some say, is all they know about the subject erroneous. Following is a description of the way children of this age understand the five concepts of death:

Irreversibility is the best understood concept at pre-kindergarten age. About 50 % of the children understood it correctly and answered that the dead can not return to life, whether they have been buried or not.

Finality: Children at this age find it easier to grasp finality in processes such as sight, hearing and motion, but have difficulty in grasping finality in complex processes such as sensation, thought and consciousness. The majority of kindergarteners (75 %) understood the tangible aspects of death (the dead do not see or hear) but only about 25 % of this age group understood the intangible aspects (the dead do not feel).

This is the cause of the erroneous beliefs many children had on the subject of sensation of the dead. These children said that the dead feel pain, since what they died of — accidents, war, illness — surely caused them pain. Such answers reveal a childish way of thinking and lack of sufficient information on the subject.

Causality: Understanding of the causality of death develops later than understanding of its irreversibility and its finality. Most pre-kindergarten children are able to give at least one reason for death, such as illness or accident, but most pre-kindergarten children are unable to grasp old age as being an important cause of death, just as they are unable to grasp the idea that all people grow old (see following paragraph). Children of this age group gave various erroneous answers as to the causes of death, such as headache or being sad etc.

Old age: Old age and its connection to death constitutes a difficult subject for pre-kindergarten children to grasp. Only about 25 %

of this age group understood the concept well enough to answer that all people grow old. One third of this group understood that all people grow old, but excluded themselves from the process of aging. This answer may indicate incomplete conceptualization of the concept of aging, but more probably it points at a defense mechanism of denial. This mechanism serves to reduce the anxiety of the child, who knows that all people grow old and die. When the child is emotionally more mature, he is able to distinguish between his fear of growing old and his intellectual understanding of the subject.

Inevitability: Inevitability is a difficult concept for children of this age to grasp and very few understand it well. Most children perceive death as being caused by random causes and therefore they think that it can be avoided. A child will think, for instance, that if death is caused by accidents, we can avoid it if we are careful, just as we can avoid death from illness if we take the necessary precautions.

Even children who understand the concept of aging, don't necessarily grasp all its implications – i.e., the inevitability of death.

As has been mentioned, one of the interesting findings of the study, as shown by these data, contradicts the commonly held belief that 4-5 year-olds understand death as it relates to animals better than death as it relates to humans. This study found the opposite to be true: Children understand less about the death of animals, even familiar animals, such as dogs. This has important implications for the kind of explanations given to children of this age.

As to the comparison of two groups of children based on the educational background of their parents:

Children from better educated families show a better understanding of death, both human and animal. The gap is particularly conspicuous where the death of animals is concerned. Children of both groups show difficulty in understanding the concept of aging and the connection between old age and death. However, while 85 % of pre-kindergarten children from well educated families grasped the irreversibility of death, the majority of children from poorly educated families said that a dead person can return to life.

The less abstract way of thinking of children from poorly educated families was also apparent in their answers regarding the finality of death. An interesting finding in this matter is that they understood the more concrete aspects of death better than the other group, and accepted the finality in such tangible functions as motion, speech and sight. They do not, however, understand finality as it relates to more abstract functions, such as consciousness and sensation. There is also a pronounced difference between the two groups in the erroneous answers they gave. For all five concepts of death, as related to humans, and particularly for irreversibility and inevitability, children from poorly educated families gave more erroneous answers, or were unable to give answers at all.

B. Kindergarten Age

A most striking development in the understanding of the concepts of death occurs during the transition between pre-kindergarten and kindergarten age. The concept that kindergarten children have of death is significanthy more mature than that of pre-kindergarten children. All the interviewers taking part in the study were impressed by the difference between the two age groups in the attitudes to the subject. Kindergarteners were able to define death, albeit in a concrete manner and relating to only one aspect of death ("not alive"; "an old person who died"); they exhibit more confidence when giving answers, show interest in the subject and many tell about their own relevant experiences – a cat that was run over, a relative who passed away, etc. Most children in this age group show a mature grasp of death, particularly in two of its aspects; *irreversibility* and *finality*. (These two concepts were also the best understood by the pre-kindergarten age group.)

Children's perception of the *causality* of death is evidence of their concrete way of thinking. Though most children were able to name one or more causes of death, very few spontaneously gave *old age* as a cause. Though 2/3 of the children had a clear conception of biological sequence (most of them said that all people age), many still did not grasp the connection between old age and death. One of the most remarkable and surprising findings in connection with conceptualization of causality was that none of the children participating in the study, whether of pre-kindergarten or kindergarten age, gave moral causes for death, such as 'Danny's father died because he used to beat Danny.' Neither did the children cite wish as a cause of death. There was no answer such as 'Daddy died because someone cursed him and wished him dead'.

60 % of the kindergarteners had a good conception of age (as compared to 25 % of pre-kindergarten children). This represents the greatest 'jump' in conceptualization found in the study. In addition, there were children who were able to conceptualize old age properly, but who excluded themselves from the aging process. About 1/3 of the children from well educated families understood aging in animals, while children from poorly educated families had difficulty in applying the concept of aging to animals.

As was observed in the pre-kindergarten age group, among kindergarteners, too, there is a connection between the concept of biological sequence and the maturation of the concept of inevitability of death, which, for this age group too, is the most difficult to grasp. Only about 50 % of the children understood that death is inevitable and befalls all living persons. About 25 % of the children excluded themselves or their relatives from those destined to die, or put off death to a very distant old age, e.g., 'I will die only when I'm 100 years old'. The gap between the answers given for human death and those given for animals death by the 5-6 age group (human death is, as mentioned before, better understood) is narrower than the gap in the 4-5 age group but it is not yet completely closed.

As to comparison between children from well educated families and those from poorly educated families; as can be seen from graph 1 (page 236) during the transition from pre-kindergarten age to kindergarten age great progress occurs in the way children from both groups perceive death. However, while the first group progresses from a partial to a fuller understanding of the concept of death, the second group progresses from an erroneous conception to a partial understanding; thus the relative gap in understanding between the two groups remains.

C. First Grade

The progress in a child's understanding of the concept of death continues between his sixth and seventh year, though it is slower than that made between his 4th and 5th year.

Most children in this age group (87 %) understand the concept of *irreversibility* and only a small minority (10 %) perceives the act of burial as being the cause of irreversibility. These children stated that a person who has been buried cannot return to life, though one who has not been buried 'might still be saved' somehow.

At this stage it becomes possible to try to explain irreversibility in biological terms, since first graders more or less understand the functioning of the parts of the body and the impossibility of returning a function once it has stopped.

The concept of *finality*, too, is clear to most of the children (74 %), particularly as related to the more concrete aspects, such as motion, but also as related to the more abstract aspects, such as consciousness and sensation.

Very few children are unable to grasp that finality relates to sensation also. Beginning with first grade there is slow progress towards a full understanding of the concept of finality, which is achieved in fourth grade.

The transition to first grade is the stage at which the greatest progress is made in understanding the concept of *causality*. This progress is part of the general process of maturation of the concept as it applies to all aspects in the child's world, including death. At this stage, as has been mentioned, magical thinking ceases and is replaced by an understanding of cause and effect.

A conspicuous finding of the study is that children in this age-group begin giving biological explanations for death, such as 'one dies when one's heart stops'. Along with beginning to use biological terms, children at this age also show a better developed understanding of the process of biological sequence and the majority (77 %) understand the significance of *old age*.

Nevertheless, few children spontaneously gave old age as one of the causes of death. This is apparently due to what Kastenbaum refers to as 'children's limited comprehension of the future'. According to Kastenbaum, it is only in adolescence that the concept of aging becomes incorporated in the immediate substance of a person's world. Up to this age, though a child may understand what old age is, the concept is emotionally distant from him. 63 % of the first graders were also able to understand the concept of *inevitability*.

The gap in understanding between human death and animal death narrows in this age group, although first graders will find it difficult to generalize their conception of old age and inevitability of death, enough to include animals. This narrowing of the gap in children's conceptualization of human death and animal death apparently reflects the process of generalization which the children's concept of death undergoes at the age of 6-7. 25 % of the children in this age group spontaneously answered the question 'who dies?' with 'all people and animals'.

To summarize this stage, it may be said that the age of 6-7 marks the transition from a childish to a more mature conceptualization of death. But although many children aged 6-7 understand and generalize each of the five concepts of death and received perfect scores on the questionnaire, others still had difficulty in generalizing some concepts, even though they understood most of its aspects.

As for comparison between children from poorly educated families with those from well educated families, the progress made by the first group between kindergarten and first grade (an average of 3 points) is greater than the progress made by the second group (an average of 2 points), thus narrowing the gap between the two groups.

Most first graders from well educated families have a sound conception of death, in all concepts related to humans, save causality. The great majority (over 88 %) got a perfect score.

The concept of old age is not yet spontaneously brought up by this age group, but when questioned about it directly, the majority show full comprehension of it (92 % of the children got a perfect score).

Children from poorly educated families showed progress in their understanding of the concepts of old age and irreversibility. On the other hand, they made little progress in understanding the finality of death and its inevitability. Like the other group, these children failed to bring up old age in their answers spontaneously, but when questioned about it directly they showed progress in their under-standing of the concept.

The expansion of the concept of death to include animals, particularly in the concepts of old age and inevitability is manifest in both groups. However, while 77 % of the children from well educated families got perfect scores on old age and 66 % got perfect scores on inevitability, only about 22 % of the children from poorly educated homes got perfect scores on old age and only 40 % got perfect scores on inevitability. Moreover, many children in this group lacked the slightest understanding of the above two concepts. It seems that these children are capable of forming a sound concept of human death before they are capable of doing so for animal death. In addition, the gap between them and the other group is greater when it comes to animal death.

The attitudes toward death proved to be different in the two different population groups. Children from well educated families talked about death with a greater degree of confidence, showed a greater willingness to talk about the subject, and spontaneously added details from their own experience. Children from poorly educated families were more reserved, answered less confidently, and only few of them added examples or details of their own.

D. Second Grade

All children participating in the study showed continued devel-opment in their concept of death between first and second grade. Their progress in conceptualizing human death is more marked than the progress made in conceptualizing animal death. Over 90 % of the children correctly conceptualize the *finality* of death, its *irreversibility* and *old age* as related to humans.

There is great progress in comprehension of *causality*. Though even younger children are able to give at least one correct cause of death, they find it difficult to understand *old age* as a cause of death, just like illness or war. About 1/3 of the second graders in the study spontaneously named old age as a cause of death, compared to a mere 7 % in first grade.

Comprehension of old age and the *inevitability* of death, when related to animals, still lags behind comprehension of the same concepts as related to humans. The gap in comprehension of these two concepts when related to humans and to animals underscores the difference in the development of conceptualization of death between children from well educated families and those from poorly educated families. Children from well educated families who have achieved a good understanding of the concept of human death also show progress in their understanding of animal death. In contrast, children from poorly educated families still show a marked gap between their understanding of human death and their understanding of animal death. This gap is not the same for all the concepts, but is particularly marked for the concepts of causality and old age.

This means that children from poorly educated families have difficulty in forming a comprehensive understanding of death as a phenomenon related to the sequence of life in general, and resulting from biological processes beyond any single cause.

It should be noted that from the second grade up, children begin giving biological explanations for death, particularly its finality ('a dead person can not see because his eyes are no longer living', or 'he is dead because his heart died'). Such explanations came largely from the group of children of well educated parents.

It is interesting to note that from second grade on, the children in the study spontaneously referred to the subject of religion (though the population studied was not from religious schools).

The matter of faith emerged in the answers of a small number of children to questions regarding the irreversibility of death. However, while children from well educated families differentiated between fact and faith, children from poorly educated families did not. Some of the former group answered the question "Can a dead person return to life?" with "No, but some people believe that the dead will return to life when the Messiah comes". On the other hand, some of the latter answered the question with a straight forward affirmative: "Yes, the dead can return to life when the Messiah comes, and then they will come home and we'll be able to talk to them."

With the exception of a small number of such answers, the way the children in the study perceived death was in no way affected by the Jewish faith. All the children participating in the study were attending secular public schools.

E. Third and Fourth Grade

Since by second grade most children have a fair understanding of the concepts of death, the progress made between second and third grade and between third and fourth grade is slight. It is safe to say that by third and fourth grade most children comprehend the phenomenon of death, with the exception of the concept of *causality*, which is still only partly understood. In addition, a small number of children at this age still understand *animal death* only incompletely.

In this age group the gap between children from well educated families and those from poorly educated families is gradually closed. This is true with one exception: There are still some children from poorly educated families who fail to reach a fair understanding of animal death, particularly as related to old age.

Moreover, it is interesting to note that only the group of children from well educated families scored 98 % on the concepts of irreversibility and finality. The other group had lower scores. What this means is that a teacher can assume that a fourth grade class will have a good understanding of the concept of death, with the exception of a few individual children who may have only a partial understanding of some of its aspects.

Chapter 8: Some General Conclusions on the Concepts of Death Held by Israeli Children

Following are some general conclusions, which though they are based on the findings detailed in the previous section, go beyond them in their generalization (it may be assumed that these conclusions also apply to age groups below the pre-kindergarten age group, which were not included in this study. On the basis of an additional pilot study on three year old children.) The first conclusion is significant mainly in the theoretical sphere, while the others have important pratical applications.

1. Kindergarteners in Israel know more about human death than they do about animal death. Their level of conceptualizing human death is developmentally about one year more advanced than their level of conceptualizing animal death.

This is a somewhat surprising conclusion, since on the basis of what is known about a child's general development and on the basis of the order of the questions on the questionnaire, the opposite results, i.e. an earlier conceptualization of animal death might have been expected.

All the children were first asked the questions concerning human death and afterwards the questions concerning animal death. Although the interviewers refrained from giving any clues as to whether the answers given were right or wrong, the very fact that a child's attention was fixed on the subject (of human death) might have caused some transfer, so that the answers he gave about human death might have led him to generalize and to form conclusions about animal death, thus improving his answers on animal death.

Based on what we know about a child's development, children, particularly very young children, might have been expected to be able to conceptualize animal death better than, and earlier than, human death, and that due to several causes:

a) From an early age, children encounter death in the animal world — when they see a dead bird or a dead dog, for instance. Such experiences could advance their understanding of animal death.

b) Young children are emotionally closer to the animal world than they are to adults; their emotional identification with animals is a common and recognized phenomenon. Thus it might have been expected that they would have a better understanding of death in a world closer to them.

c) Death is a subject which is likely to arouse in a child fears and anxieties about himself and those near and dear to him. Therefore, it might have been expected that children would find it easier to talk about the death of animals than about the death of humans, and that their answers on the former subject might be better.

d) It may be supposed that adults find it easier to talk to a child about animal death than about human death, and that, therefore, the explanations he hears from adults concerning the death of animals would be more exact than those concerning the death of humans.

The findings of our study contradict all the above assumptions, which are common among many adults — parents and teachers alike. It appears that a child's conceptualization of death develops separately for each of two separate spheres: A child understands human death earlier because he apparently understands human life earlier. His conceptualization of life and death in the animal world apparently develops later than, and separately from, his conceptualization of human life and death. (This has to be studied empirically)

According to our findings, the gap in conceptualization between human death and animal death is particularly marked on the concepts of old age, causality and inevitability. Kindergarteners find it difficult to understand that dogs grow old, that the aging process holds true for them too and that they must eventually die, too.

On the other hand, on the concepts of irreversibility and finality children's understanding of human death and animal death were on the same level. This is so perhaps because these are the easiest concepts for children to understand. Another possible reason for this may lie in our impression that children do not look upon a dead dog in the same way they look upon a dead human. A dead human is a human body, still human though in a different state, while a dead dog becomes an inanimate object. Therefore it is clear why a child will say "a dead dog will not return to be a dog" or "a dead cat can not feel", since dead animals have become for him inanimate objects to be discarded in the trash can. for children that do not own a dog. In other words, it is possibly the above erroneous conceptualization

53

of animal death that is responsible for the correct conceptualization of these particular aspects of death.

The conclusion that children know less about animal death than they do about human death has clear implications. It indicates that in explaining death to a child, we should concentrate on human death, which he understands better.

2. There is a gap in the level of conceptualizing death, in all age groups, between children from well educated families and those from poorly educated families. However, the curve of the development of their conceptualization of death is similar for all children.

Many researchers believe that the development of a child's conceptualization of death is influenced by two principal factors: The child's age and his I.Q. Since the study showed a clear statistical correlation between a child's age and intelligence and his conceptualization of death, it is clear why there were marked differences in the level of conceptualization of death, between children from well educated families, whose intelligence level is relatively higher, and children from poorly educated families, whose intelligence level is relatively lower, on the average.

However, despite this gap it is important to note that the sequence in which conceptualization of death develops is similar in all children, of all levels of intelligence. All children, no matter what their background, first conceptualize the irreversibility of death and its finality, then they conceptualize causality, and last, old age and inevitability. All children, no matter what their background, comprehend human death before they comprehend animal death. The quantiative difference between the two different background groups lies in the fact that children from well educated families are about one year ahead of children from poorly educated families in their level of conceptualizing death. That is to say, the children of the latter group require an additional year of cognitive development before they can catch up with the level of conceptualization of children in the former group.

As for the qualitative aspect, we found that the difference between the two groups lies in the fact that children from poorly educated homes have more difficulty in understanding the abstract aspects of death, such as the cessation of sensation or old age in animals.

In terms of application, this conclusion means that there is no need for a different kind of explanation to be given to children from an educationally deprived background. When the subject of death is raised in a heterogeneous class, the teacher need not fear that these children will have substantial difficulties in understanding. As for homogeneous classes, the nature of the discussion of the subject can be similar for all classes, but the teacher should remember that children from well educated families are about one year ahead in conceptualization of death.

3. A child's environment greatly affects the development of his conceptualization of death. This development can be advanced and accelerated by appropriate intervention.

Like many other spheres in a child's development, the development of his conceptualization of death depends on the interaction of internal conditions such as his I.Q., his rate of cognitive maturation, his emotional development, etc., and external environmental conditions such as the influence of his family, friends and society at large.

A "sufficient intelligence level" and a certain emotional maturity (both 'internal' factors) are required for a good understanding of the concept of death and an effective way of dealing with the phenomenon. Our study indeed found direct evidence of the influence of the variables of age and intelligence on conceptualization of death. On the other hand, comparison of our findings with findings of similar studies conducted in other countries shows that the environmental conditions in which a child grows up greatly affect his understanding of death. Our study shows that Israeli children, who grow up in a society in which there is much awareness of and involvement with the subject of death, are ahead of children in other countries in the level of their conceptualization of death. Would it be possible, then, by means of reinforcement of the environmental factor through appropriate educational guidance, to advance the Israeli child's conceptualization of death even further? What if pre-kindergarten children, who have formed a partial concept of death, were offered the opportunity to talk about death freely and openly, if their questions on the subject were answered frankly, if they received explanations suitable to their age, about the aspects of death they don't yet understand and reinforcement of the aspects they already know about? Could we thereby advance the level of their conceptualization of death so that many understand it by the age of four and that most children reach a full understanding of the concept by first or second grade? These questions can be answered only on the basis of experimental studies.

It must be pointed out that the children in our study were growing up in an environment which does not provide sufficient and appropriate explanation on the subject of death. It may be assumed that being provided with such explanation would help the children to make the most of their intellectual capacities and to advance their conceptualization of death − each child according to his individual ability, of course.

In addition to the advancement of their understanding of death on the intellectual-cognitive level the children would benefit on the emotional level from the opportunity to talk about death. In such talks they could express their fears and anxieties and could receive an adult's reinforcement of the idea that death is a natural phenomenon and that it is permissible, and even desirable, to talk about it.

Such emotional experience will help the child to deal with occurrences of death in his close environment in the future and will help orphaned children to feel more at ease in the company of their peers.

In conclusion, we recommend that a comprehensive educational program be implemented in schools and kindergartens, with the aim of advancing children's understanding of death, on the intellectual as well as on the emotional level. Such a program would be based on what the child already knows based on the questionnaire for Examination of Human and Animal Death Conceptualization and would include direct conversations, story-telling, etc. Any adult (whether psychologist, teacher, counselor, or parent) can talk to children about death and help them deal with sad but inevitable phenomenon and explain concepts.

Part Two:

HELPING THE ORPHANED* CHILD TO DEAL WITH DEATH

The subject of death is brought into the school not only because many children are preoccupied with it or because many have encountered it directly (a neighbor dying, for instance), but also because in many schools there are children who have been personally affected by the death of someone in their immediate family (a parent, grandparent or sibling). These children require special attention from their teacher and their classmates, taking into account the needs arising from their special situation.

The teacher should undoubtedly play a central part in helping the orphaned child adjust to a new reality – life without his dead parent. However, many teachers claim that their training as teachers has not prepared them to deal with the problems of the orphan. They feel that they have no idea of the needs of the orphan while he is undergoing the process of mourning and adjustment. Furthermore, they do not know how to treat an occurrence of death in the framework of the classroom and how to prepare the class to receive the orphaned child.

This chapter will endeavor to deal with this subject in detail, taking into account the problems and difficulties in the readjustment of the orphan, describing the various stages of the mourning process, and emphasizing the role of the teacher in helping the orphan to readjust.

---

*   In this book, the word *orphan* refers to a child who lost his father or mother by death.

Chapter 1: Problems in the Readjustment of the Orphan –
A Review of the Literature

Many books and studies deal with the role and importance of the parent in the process of the socialization of the young child and the influence of the parent on the development of the child. In contrast, there are few studies dealing with how the death of a parent affects young children.

The nuclear family is characteristically small so that the parents constitute almost the only source of dependence and identification for the child and he often turns only to them for intimacy. The father and the mother represent different role models, interaction and internalization of these models help the child to shape various aspects of his character.

Clearly both parents play an important part in the development of the child. They serve as objects of identification and role models and they provide a frame of reference for behavior with the opposite sex. A normal process of identification – which depends on the regular presence of both parents – enables the child to function as a whole personality and to learn to function effectively in the various roles required of him.

In the professional literature much reference is made to the effect the death of a parent has on the future development of the orphan. Hinton (1967) points out that the death of a parent may have a drastic effect on the development of a child's personality. Nevertheless, it is difficult to determine which of the many material and emotional changes occurring in the life of the orphan is the main cause of the deviation in his development. A study of the factors affecting the child together with an effort to prevent them, might therefore forestall various phenomena which the orphan may suffer at a later time, such as a tendency toward depression, sociopathic behavior and self-destructiveness.

In his discussion of the factors affecting the orphan's adjustment Wolfenstein (1963) claims that the orphaned child, who has until the death of his parent viewed him as part of himself, now feels incomplete and inadequate when he compares himself to other children. This may lead to an inferiority complex and a syndrome which Wolfenstein calls a combination of envy and melancholia. Isaacs (1950) maintains that the orphan develops depressive patterns of behavior, a low self image, self-hate, and a lack of confidence in the future. In addition, the orphan may show a tendency to run away from responsibility while at the same time developing a sensitivity to what adults think of him. Hilgard (1965) deals with environmental influences before and after mourning and points out the following pathological phenomena occurring in orphans:

a) Developing an over-dependence on the surviving parent, which is in most cases stimulated by the needs of the parent himself.

b) A tendency to relive the traumatic experience on certain dates.

Sears (1951) found that children who grew up without a father were more aggressive than children who grew up with their fathers. He believes that the absence of a father creates in the child a need for affection and security. When the need is not satisfied, the child develops fantasies and idealizations together with anger and agressiveness.

In her article on children whose fathers died Isaacs (1950) discusses the development of anti-social behavior in orphans. In her opinion, the orphan may lie more, cheat, disturb lessons, steal, and be generally undisciplined. He adopts these negative behavior patterns as a means of searching for a strong substitute father figure to discipline him.

M. Lipshitz (1974), too, speaks of behavior patterns which are characteristic of orphans in situations outside the family. Orphans show less interest than other children in the teacher and in the subject matter. Some orphans showed less positive interest in their friends, relative to other children. Teachers, also, tend to describe orphans as different. They look upon orphans as either "too mature" or "too childish". Lipshitz believes that teachers may perceive orphans as children absorbed in their own personal problems and therefore less willing to participate in what is happening around them. Moreover, the absence of a father affects the cognitive adjustment and learning ability of a child. Brown (1966) found a significant difference of 8 points between the I.Q. of children who had no fathers and those in the control group.

A study conducted in Israel on "The Adjustment of Fatherless Children to Elementary School" (S. Smilansky and T. Diksel, 1977) shows the scholastic achievements of orphans in Israel to be significantly lower than those of the control group. It appears that orphans do not utilize all, or even most, of their intellectual capacity in their studies.

Schlesinger (1970) notes that even when the orphan shows no extreme behavioral deviations, such as delinquency, he may be expected to have problems of adjustment in his school and among his peers who, not having experienced a traumatic event such as the loss of a parent, are not sensitive to the problems of the orphans.

Parents of orphaned children and members of the educational staff in the community should therefore receive guidance in dealing with the problems which arise in the orphan's process of adjustment. The community, the school, and the peer group also need guidance in dealing with the orphan. A study, (Smilansky, 1977) by means of a sociometric test, of the social position of orphans in their classes reveals that orphans are significantly more rejected by their classmates than children of the control group. This is surprising, since it was to be expected that the children in the orphan's class would have been told by both their parents and their teachers to be especially sensitive to the orphan, on no account to reject him, and to try to help him and ease his pain as far as possible.

The emotional adjustment of orphans, as judged by their teachers, is inferior to that of the control group (Smilansky 1977). Orphans show poorer adjustment in most of the areas that are components of the term emotional adjustment. Significant differences were found in the indices of self confidence, mood and appearance. That is, in the judgment of their teachers it was clearly distinguishable that the orphans were less self confident, more shy, more reticent, more easily discouraged, and given to more extreme moods — mostly sadness and depression. Their absorption with their own loss and with death affects not only their self confidence and their mood, but also, in their teachers' judgment, their appearance, as compared with children in the control group.

In conclusion, the scholastic, social, and emotional adjustment of orphans of elementary school age is significantly poorer than that of children in a control group, consisting of children in the orphan's classes who come from a similar socio-economic background. It seems that these findings are the result of a faulty working through of the mourning process. Psychological literature emphasizes factors which affect a child's ability to mourn and to readjust:

1. Adults in the environment, e.g., family, teachers, social workers, psychologists, etc. can aid the child to mourn and to work through the various stages of mourning, thus opening the possibility for readjustment.

2. Knowledge about and understanding of the concepts of death.

Chapter 2: The Help of Adults as a Factor in a Child's Mourning Process

The crisis of a beloved person's death is one of the hardest experiences a person can undergo. Death means a permanent parting from a person to whom one is attached and on whom one depends. While the physical parting is immediate, the process of emotional severance is long and painful. The mourner experiences various painful feelings: sorrow and longing for the deceased, a sense of lack and incompleteness, guilt, anger, directed either at the deceased or at others who "caused" his/her death. Along with such feelings the process of mourning is characterized by a great deal of absorption with the deceased — looking at his/her pictures, reminiscing about experiences shared with him/her, telling anecdotes about him/her etc.

The process of mourning, although difficult and painful, is indispensable, particularly so for children, whose toleration for pain is low. The fact of physical separation from the deceased remains, and the child must undergo a reorganization of his personality in order to adjust to life without him/her. A sound mourning enables the child to achieve an emotional separation from the deceased by means of a process of internalizing the image of the deceased parent and turning it into part of the mourner's personality. In this way the child regains the libidinal energy which he/she invested in the deceased, so that he/she can now invest it in new objects, and form new emotional relationships.

Like adults, children are not able to go through the mourning process alone and to deal with their mourning, in its various phases, on their own. Mourning is a socio-psychological interaction. The bereaved child's mourning process and his/her subsequent readjustment depend on the wisdom, the understanding and the sensitivity of the adults in his environment: the members of his family, his teachers, various professionals with whom he comes in contact, and other adults. The child is dependent on adults both for their allowing him/her to mourn and for their help in working through his/her mourning.

Adults play an important role in the orphan's mourning process, both as models for imitation of mourning behavior (which is instrumental in sound adjustment) and as a source of help and guidance, so that he/she may come through the mourning process in a manner that will lead to his/her readjustment. An adult may help in the mourning process in various ways. He/she may lessen the pain through his sympathy, help the child to accept the finality of the loss of his parent, cognitively and emotionally adjusting to a new reality. He/she may help construct a new reality for the child, talking about the deceased and giving the child the opportunity to express his/her feelings and become aware of their significance. He/she may show understanding for the orphan's wishes, relieving the orphan's anxiety about the future, etc.

Chapter 3: The School as a Source of Help to the Orphan

Many researchers (Mitchell, 1966, Yudkin, 1960, Redl, 1951) found that children's attitude to death is influenced by the attitudes of adults significant in their lives. Who, then, are these adults? If, as we have suggested, the teacher belongs to this category, should he intervene in the mourning process of children in his class, or is mourning a family matter in the realm of interaction between the widow/widower and the orphan alone? The surviving parent undoubtedly plays an important part in the mourning process of his/her child. However, he/she often does not know how to behave with his/her children, how to answer their questions, and to what extent to allow them to participate in the mourning. Since he/she has not experienced such a painful situation before, the bereaved parent needs the guidance of someone with a professional background in education and psychology, someone who understands the child's needs. Training teachers to deal with this subject and expanding their awareness of it would prepare them to fulfill the role of counselor in such a situation. Moreover, it must be remembered that at this stage the surviving parent is not always able to give maximum attention to the orphans. He/she has just gone through a difficult and painful experience and he/she is absorbed in his/her own grief and is himself/herself in need of help from others in order to come through his/her mourning and become readjusted. The child, on the other hand, needs the counseling and guidance of adults in many matters, especially at such a difficult time.

For this reason the role of the teacher as a significant figure of authority is so important to the orphan. Unlike his/her parent, the teacher is not so deeply involved in the painful situation and he/she is therefore able to help the orphan, in place of or in addition to his parent, and to aid him/her in reconstructing his/her life.

The teacher's help should focus on two principal areas:

1. Direct help to the child through sympathy, understanding, and initiation of talks on subjects that trouble him/her. The teacher can help the child to gain better concepts of death and acknowledge his/her anxiety about the future.

2. Counseling and help with the interpersonal interaction of the bereaved child with the other children in his/her class. The class, it must be remembered, can be a constructive and supportive framework for the orphan. The large number of children who have not suffered the loss of a parent as well as children who have themselves suffered bereavement can offer a variety of support. It is important that these conditions be fully exploited by the teacher. Without a thorough understanding of how children, bereaved and non-bereaved, conceptualize death and without an awareness of the child's needs during the process of mourning and following it, the teacher will find it difficult to offer support to the bereaved child.

Chapter 4: A Child's Mourning Process and Teachers' Help

The death of a beloved person is a painful and traumatic experience which imposes changes on the child's inner world. These changes take place in the course of the mourning process. They constitute a detachment from the deceased after acceptance of the fact of his death, on the cognitive as well as on the emotional level. Adjustment to a new reality based on the development of a new self-image, which does not include the deceased and which allows the child to divert his/her emotional energy to establishing a new emotional relationship with those around him/her must be achieved. The child must go through all the phases of mourning in order to achieve an emotional detachment from the deceased and to fashion his new world. Although most researchers found that children mourn from a very young age, a child can not begin and complete a mourning process withoug help from adults.

For a better understanding of the essence of a child's mourning, the three phases of the mourning process: acceptance of the fact of death, working through the grief, and adjustment to a new reality — will be described. Adults, and teachers in particular, play a part in each of these three phases.

Phase 1: *Acceptance of the fact of Death*

Acceptance of the fact of death comprises two factors: cognitive understanding and emotional acceptance. Cognitive comprehension is imperative for emotional acceptance. Acceptance in its wider sense, including both its factors, is imperative for the next phases of mourning, which will be described later.

The child must be informed of the death as soon as his family knows of it. He/she should be told by someone he trusts (e.g., mother, teacher, aunt) and in a clear and unequivocal manner. Any effort to hide the painful fact from the child, partly or wholly, may impede his subsequent readjustment. However, the child should be told the truth gently, with sensitivity and empathy.

When a parent dies, something crucial has changed in the child's life – one of his/her parents has gone from him never to return. The child must accept this hard fact and begin reconstructing his world, a new world which does not include his deceased parent. Without reliable knowledge of his parent's death the child cannot go through a proper mourning. Even if his/her family later on tries to correct matters by telling the child the whole truth, the child will find it difficult to accept it. Based on his/her experience that what adults say cannot be relied on, he/she will develop explanations using imagination, fantasy, magical and wishful thinkings, and refuse to accept the fact that he/she is never to see his parent again.

Even when the child has received reliable information concerning his/her parent's death, he/she still must go through certain processes in order to achieve emotional acceptance of the fact of death. He/she must understand and accept the finality of death and its irreversibility.

Interviews with adults who were orphaned in childhood confirm and illustrate what has been said above. (see interviews in Part V of this book, page 141).

Several of the interviewed subjects referred to the importance of the orphan being notified of his parent's death as soon as possible and as clearly and unequivocally as possible. "It is important to tell the child the truth, and in a clear and concrete manner, though without too many painful details", said a 26-year-old subject whose mother died when he was six years old.

"A child ought to be told of his parent's death immediately; nothing should be hidden or glossed over. If the child wants to know specific details, they should be provided. He must know what happened immediately so that he can confront the new situation and begin adjusting to it... He will have to go through all these stages sooner or later and there is no point in putting it off. In any case, the child has a right to know what has happened to his parent." These are the words of a 35-year-old woman whose father died when she was a child, 9 years old.

An additional argument is provided by a 23-year-old whose father died in an accident when she was eight: "No matter at what age, a child should be told the truth, and given an explanation. Children ought to be taught that death is an inseparable part of life, and inevitable..."

Adults often refrain from telling a child the truth out of a wish to shield him from the bitter truth and due to their own bewilderment and fear of the child's reaction. This attitude is wrong and undesirable in the opinions of the interviewed subjects, who experienced the loss of a parent as children. A 28-year-old whose father died when he was a teenager and who suffered from the family's unwillingness to speak about anything connected with the death, stated, "A child should be told of his parent's death without recourse to such stories as 'Daddy has gone away for a while'. Even at pre-kindergarten age a child should be told that his father is dead, and if he asks what that means, he should be given an explanation with reference to a dead animal that he may have seen, or some similar experience."

"The fact of a parent's death must not be hidden from the child", said a 17-year-old subject whose mother died of an illness when he was six. Neither should the notification of the child be put off, because the longer it is put off, the more difficult it becomes to tell the child... It is better to inform him immediately, to tell him everything and to answer his questions honestly."

Another subject, a 30-year-old woman whose mother died when she was eleven-years-old, told of an undesirable personal experience: "Nobody told me exactly what had happened. I felt that everyone was very sad, but no one explained to me... I was bewildered and dazed... Finally my aunt said "Your mother has passed away". I didn't understand what 'passed away' meant and I didn't know what exactly had happened because I didn't dare ask."

In summary, it may be stated that the personal experience of those who lost a parent when they were children, teaches how important it is to notify the child of the death as soon as possible and as honestly and clearly as possible. Euphemisms should not be used. The child should be told the truth, but the truth should be phrased according to the child's age and level of understanding. It is important to let the child feel that it is permissible to ask any question and to express any feeling.

Child's presence at the funeral

The funeral, and particularly the lowering of the casket into the grave, can illustrate to the child the finality of death. The child's presence at the time of the lowering of the casket into the grave and its being covered over with earth can serve to dispel doubts that might arise. If the child is not present at the funeral, he/she may later be troubled by doubts such as whether it was really his/her father who was buried or whether his father might now be somewhere else and if so whether the child ought perhaps to look for him. When the child sees the lowering of the casket into the grave, he/she may accept the finality of death as a fact. Even when a child is not present at the funeral, it is important that the funeral be described to him/her in detail, particularly the facts related to the lowering of the casket into the grave. Such a description will aid the child in a cognitive acceptance of the finality of death, which, as has been pointed out, is crucial to its emotional acceptance. Adults frequently fear that the painful emotional expressions during the rites of mourning, (the funeral, etc.) might shock the child. The resulting decision to shield him from these experiences and allow him/her to continue with the routine of his/her life is misguided and erroneous. The child must realize that something essential has changed in his/her life. This 'something' is painful and difficult, and that is why the people around him/her are reacting emotionally. The child's former routine must not be allowed to continue undisturbed, since something disturbing has happened, and his/her life will not be the same as before.

"Children should be taken to the funeral. It is very important that the family should be together during difficult moments. The mourning family should be together at all times... Before the funeral the children should be prepared and told exactly what happens so that they do not get a shock and begin thinking all kinds of thoughts ... If the child doesn't want to attend the funeral he should not be forced to attend, but he can be told what exactly happens at the funeral." These are the words of a sixteen-year-old who lost her father, and they summarize all the main points: The importance of letting the child participate in the funeral, and on the other hand, flexibility and sensitivity to his/her wishes, his/her age and his/her personality.

A number of those interviewed gave the main arguments for having orphaned children take part in the funeral. "Children should be taken to the funeral." "The funeral actualizes the finality of death and helps the child to understand what happened." "The funeral helps the child to understand the significance of the calamity". "The funeral constitutes a rite of final parting, and that is important". "Things become clearer". "The child sees with his own eyes that his father, or mother, is no longer alive, and that is important. However, an adult should explain to the child during the funeral exactly what is happening".

Some subjects speak of feelings of regret and guilt that the orphan later has about not having attended his parent's funeral. "One of the things about my father's death that troubles me still is the fact that I did not attend the funeral. I returned from abroad one day later and I was notified on the telephone. Actually it was not a complete surprise because he had been ill..., but still it was hard for me to accept because I had hoped to come in time to see him once more. I still feel guilty about not having been at the funeral..." These are the words of a subject whose father died when he was a teenager.

"Children should be taken to the funeral so that they will not feel that they have betrayed their parent and have not properly parted from him", said a 27-year-old subject whose mother died when he was six. He was left with relatives at the time of the funeral. "For a long time afterwards I used to dream that my mother was not dead and was coming back to greet me..."

"If you don't go to the funeral, you may have feelings of regret and guilt. I did not say goodbye to my father properly" said one of the subjects.

Several subjects spoke of the emotional difficulty that children experience in connection with the funeral. This difficulty may even be traumatic. However, there are ways by which adults can ease the experience for the child and prevent its undesirable effects on the child.

A subject whose mother died when she was twelve, emphasized the importance of preparing the child for the funeral: "The child should be told exactly what is about to happen." Another subject, whose father was killed in an accident when she was eight, added, "A child should participate in the funeral in order to grasp what has happened. It is undoubtedly a difficult experience, but it is one that the child should experience... It is difficult to grasp what has happened, especially if the death is sudden. The funeral ceremony makes what happened more real and helps the child to face reality... The funeral ceremony also serves as a symbol of parting".

At all events, the adults of the family or those aiding the family, are the ones who must decide whether or not to allow the orphan to participate in the funeral. The decision should not be left to the orphan, as it puts heavy and unfair pressure on him. "Such a question would only have bewildered me", explained one of the subject, whose mother died when he was six. "On one hand I would have been scared to go, but on the other hand I would have felt uncomfortable saying that I didn't want to go".

In general, therefore, it is desirable to allow the orphaned child to participate in the funeral, but on two conditions, that the funeral is preceded by suitable preparation and explanation, and that the child's age and personality are taken into consideration before the decision is made. Sometimes it may be preferable to describe the funeral to the child instead of having him attend.

Sitting with the family during the Shiv'a helps to make the child realize that a change has taken place in his/her life and prepares him/her for gradual acceptance of this change. It is, however, important that the Shiv'a be observed in the child's home, to prevent him/her from feeling that everything familiar has been taken from him/her, that he is no longer on solid ground. He/she has lost his/her parent, and that is a catastrophe, but he/she must be made to feel that he/she has not lost his/her home.

Adults who were orphaned in childhood stated, "It is desirable that the child stay at home during the Shiv'a, although he must be allowed to find relief by playing with or visiting his friends; he is, after all, having a very hard time". "The child should stay home because he should know about death and Shiv'a... he should feel that something has changed... so that he can begin adjusting to the change and accepting the new reality."

A 24-year-old subject who lost his mother when he was six states, "It is important that the child stay at home so that he can see that nothing is being hidden from him, that nothing terrible is happening. His staying at home is also important to make the child feel that he still has the rest of his family and need not part with them, in addition to having to part with his deceased parent forever."

There are cases when children are sent away from home to stay with friends or distant relatives during the time of the Shiv'a. This is done under the misconception that it will spare them pain by not subjecting them to the depressing atmosphere at home. Such a decision is undoubtedly wrong for the child, for it is precisely at this time that he/she needs the feeling of security provided by closeness to the surviving parent, siblings and other close relatives. "I think the child should stay at home because he is part of the family and should share the experience with them", says a 25-year-old subject who lost his father when he was eight.

We conducted a study (see description of this study on page 242) to establish the connection between a child's being orphaned and his understanding of finality and irreversibility, the two concepts of death which are significant during this phase of mourning. The study showed that orphans are less able to conceptualize these two aspects of death than children in the control group, who were the same age and of the same background and intelligence level. Especially prominent was the difference between the two groups in their understanding of irreversibility, with the orphans scoring significantly lower. The fact that the intellectual capacity of the orphans was not inferior to that of the control group emphasizes the orphan's need of help from adults in order to achieve a maximal comprehension of concepts which are so vital to the mourning process.

By the end of the first phase of mourning the child accepts the fact of death. He does this first on the cognitive level, after reality has furnished proof that his parent does not return, and eventually also on the emotional level. Now the second phase begins — working through the mourning.

Mother Doesn't Cry

Father's dead,
But Mother doesn't cry.
She holds up her head
And doesn't even sigh.

She has such self control
As if nothing happened at all.
Father's in his grave,
But Mother's strong and brave.
Oh, how I wish to be
As strong and brave as she
And stop this crying, crying, crying...
But I don't think I can
Hold back my tears,
Brush off my fears,
Act like a man.

The tears keep coming,
And I keep crying,
Though, please believe me,
I'm really trying
To stop.
Why can't I be
As strong and brave as she?

The Teacher's Role in the Phase of Acceptance

As mentioned in the previous section, the role that the teacher plays during the first phase of mourning, the phase in which the fact of death is accepted, may comprise various tasks. The critical act of notification, support, encouraging the bereaved child to participate in the rites of mourning, and helping him to understand the significance of death's finality and irreversibility are among these tasks. As has been said, notification of the death need not necessarily fall to the parent. Any adult who is trusted by the child can notify him/her. He/she might sometimes perform this task better than the parent, who is himself/herself dealing with the loss.

If notice of the death reaches the school while the child is there, there is no reason why the teacher should not notify the child. The manner in which the child is notified is very important. Our Studies show that the manner in which a child is notified of the death plays an important part in his/her subsequent readiness to accept the death and the new reality without the deceased.

73

If out of the good intention to spare him, the child is notified in several stages and if he is left with the impression that there may still be hope that the parent's death is not final, he/she will later find it difficult to accept the bitter truth. If the child is not told the whole truth, he/she may later feel that the part of the truth which he/she was told is unreliable too, and he/she may interpret it subjectively according to his own wishes.

It is undoubtedly very important to show sensitivity and empathy when notifying the child of a death. He/she needs support and the feeling that the teacher shares his/her pain. However, the teacher's sympathy must not affect the content of what he/she is imparting to the child, which must be clear, reliable, and unequivocal. As the teacher is less emotionally involved than the parent, he may be better able to impart the message in a desirable manner, a manner which would not have adverse effects on the child's readjustment. While sensitivity should be shown to the child's predicament, the fact that death is final and irreversible must be made clear.

The teacher must be aware of the significance of the orphan's participation in the rites of mourning and the part it plays in his acceptance of death. The teacher should, as far as possible, help the mother decide to what extent to involve the child. Moreover, it is important for the teacher himself/herself to participate in the funeral and in the Shiv'a. The importance of the teacher's participation is stressed in an article by Tikva Weinstock (1978) which was based on an interview with the mother of a 14-year-old boy who had recently been widowed:

" 'People's joys are all the same, but their sorrows are different' said Tolstoy in Anna Karenina. Each one of us, adult or child, reacts differently to pain. 'Why has father left us? Now I'm an orphan and you're a widow!' the boy kept repeating, trying to grasp this new situation. He was heartbroken. His heart ached for the dead and for the living. He was filled with anxiety, guilt and shame. Now he was branded, different. 'All the kids have fathers except me. I'm ashamed to go to school. Once there was a kid in my class whose mother died. All the kids pitied him and let him win games. I don't want to be pitied like him.' His mother tried to reason with him. 'For how long did they pity him? A week? Two weeks? Not forever.' But the boy would not go to school. He withdrew into himself and would not even allow his good friend to visit him.

His mother notified his teacher of the reasons that her son would not be coming to school. The teacher visited the boy at his home. She sat with the family for a long while. Then she sat with her student in his room for an even longer while. He opened his heart to her. He had always liked and respected her. Now she became a symbol of continued life, of the stability that remains even when the world seems to be falling apart. She told him that he was not the only one to suffer disaster, not an exception. His friends, she said, feel the need to visit him. 'I did not invite them to share happy occasions, why should they now want to share my mourning?' the boy said. The teacher explained that the visits would be good for his friends as well as for him. She tried to convince him that they would become better persons, better citizens, for trying to share someone else's pain. Then she called the students in the boy's class who lived nearest to him and asked them to visit him.

When she walked into her class the next day, the teacher did not recognize it. There was a heavy air of silence and anxiety. Even the trouble-makers made no trouble this time. The class talked about death, about mourning, about furnishing comfort. The teacher let a group of children miss the last lesson so that they could attend the funeral. She also arranged for a friend of the orphan from another class, to join them. A party that the class had planned for that day was cancelled. Some girls suggested cancelling the parties planned in other classes as well, but that suggestion was justly rejected. Only classmates, who knew the orphan, needed to participate in his grief.

Friends began coming to the orphan's home. His good friend, who had known him from infancy, came every day for the time of prayer. Another good friend came and brought his stamp album as a gift. Friends from the Scouts came in their uniforms, before or after Scouts activities. Classmates, even those who had never been to the house before, came in quietly, with bowed heads. Though they had never prayed before, except at their Bar Mitzvah ceremonies, they now felt the need to thank God for sparing them, now that they were encountering death in all its horror, at close range. But after shaking hands and some initial hesitation, his friends began showing interest in the orphan's collection of toy soldiers, exchanging stamps, playing games. In short, they indulged in the activities of normal 14-year-olds. The boy's room soon turned into a kind of club, and the boy, who was making new friends in his time of trouble almost had reason to exclaim 'I'm lucky to be an orphan'...

It was his teacher who was behind all that. Though she had never been to his house before, she now became a regular visitor there, almost a member of the family. Accompanied by another teacher, she came during her free hours at school, as well as after school, until she felt that her student was confident of his classmates' support. Nobody else could have done what she, as his teacher, had done. Though there is no replacing the loss, she made her student feel that he had friends to share his grief and to stand by him in his hour of need.

The orphan is often preoccupied with the thought that he/she is different from what he/she was before, now that he/she is an orphan. As a result he/she wonders how he/she can return to the former routine of his/her life. He/she wonders whether his/her teacher knows about his/her misfortune and how he/she will treat him/her now. He/she wonders how his/her classmates will treat him/her, whether they will behave differently towards him/her, pity him/her, or make fun of him/her. Such questions trouble the orphan and take up much of his emotional energy at a time when this energy is so necessary to him/her in accepting death.

Many orphans react to the questions that trouble them by withdrawing into themselves and refusing to let their teachers or classmates share their grief, their mourning and their doubts. The teacher's presence at the funeral and during the Shiv'a makes him/her a partner in a difficult experience, and experience that is crucial in the orphan's life, and opens a new avenue of trust in the teacher in matters related to this painful subject. In the future, the orphan will find it easier to turn to the teacher with problems stemming from the fact of his/her being an orphan because he will know that the teacher is able to give him/her factual information and because the teacher involved himself/herself in his/her mourning and shared his/her grief.

During the Shiv'a many people visit the home of the mourning family. They come to pray (in families that observe religious tradition), to comfort, to talk about the deceased, and to express their sympathy and identification. It is important to direct sympathy not only to the adult members of the family, but also to the children. A visit by teachers and classmates signifies to the orphan that his/her loss is not some mysterious secret, that his/her friends know his grief and that they want to help him by sharing it. This reduces his/her anxiety and doubts about returning to school.

Many teachers wonder whether they should talk about the deceased even when the mourning family does not do so. As we have made clear, the widow and widower do not always know just how to behave with their children, how much to tell them and how to talk to them. In this case the teacher, as an educator and a reliable authority in such matters, can serve as counselor and object of imitation to the surviving parent. His/her attitude on death and the deceased may serve to sanction open conversations about the tragedy, about the child's feelings and about difficulties he may have in adjusting to the new situation.

How Can I Return to School

We mourned my father's death.
All those who loved him came:
Family and friends,
And some without a name.

They all shook hands with mother,
And some talked to my brother,
But no one talked to me.
I'm as lonely as can be.

Here I sit alone again
And think about my grief and pain
Daddy's gone away from me,
And no one's here to comfort me.

When I think of school, I shrink.
What will all the children think?
Can they share my tragedy?
Do they care what happened to me?

They're all playing, happy, carefree,
How can I fit in again,
After being left an orphan,
After all this grief and pain?

How can I go back to school?
How can I ever play again?
How can I sing, how can I dress,
How can I raise my hand in class
Or even, sometimes, misbehave,
When my daddy's in his grave?

Although it is clear that the orphan benefits from visits of his classmates during the Shiv'a, many teachers wonder if such visits might not be harmful to the other children. In the first chapter we discussed the significance of preventive aid to children on the subject of death. A visit to a mourning family can serve as a good opportunity for mourning on a limited scale. Such a situation serves as an opportunity for talking to non-bereaved children about death. Explanations given at such a time will be effective, as the child is not deeply emotionally involved in the misfortune. Such explanations may be likened to a vaccine. As with a vaccine, the child goes through a "light case" of mourning which prepares him for dealing more effectively with future misfortunes.

Phase 2: *Working Through the Grief*

After the mourner has accepted the fact of death, a reorganization of his personality takes place, at the end of which begins the third phase of mourning — adjustment to the new situation. The phase of reorganization is characterized by intense emotional expression. There is deep grief and pain at the loss, anger and blame directed at people who had some connection to the deceased or sometimes even at the deceased himself, and guilt. During this phase it is very important to allow the child to express his feelings and to talk to him about their significance.

Wolfenstein (1966) notes that the child's tolerance of such an intense emotional state is very low and therefore he/she may try to

78

repress his/her feelings. It must be remembered that the child does not know how to act or to handle this new situation. He/she does not know to what extent it is acceptable for him/her to express his feelings and whether by doing so he/she might cause pain to his surviving parent and other relatives. He/she expects guidance about how to behave now, just as he/she has been guided by adults about how to behave in different situations until now. It is therefore important to guide the child towards expressing his/her feelings and to encourage him to do so. This can be done either through imitation, which legitimizes expression of emotions, or through talking about the deceased, about the feelings associated with death, and about the new situation that has been created because of the death.

In Grandmother's House

At grandma's things are different
There it's O.K. to cry
Grandma doesn't hold back the tears
And there, neither do I.

After we've cried together
I think I feel relief,
And grandma says, "My dear, it's O.K.,
For a boy to express his grief".

And after all the tears are dry,
And I wash the redness from my eyes,
I go back home feeling stronger.
But as soon as I feel my mother's touch
The sobs have me back within their clutch
And I feel strong no longer.

So, my friends, you see,
For an orphan-boy like me,
With all the pain and fears,
It's hard to hold back the tears.

1. *Interviews with adults who were orphaned in childhood show the importance of talking about the deceased* (see description of this study on page 141) and looking through his photographs and souvenirs.

Many of the subjects interviewed spoke of the emotional difficulties they experienced due to the atmosphere of taboo which prevailed in the family. This taboo extended to the expression of thoughts and feelings about everything connected with the deceased and his/her death. This deliberate avoidance of direct reference to the misfortune, this self-restraint, these inhibitions sometimes have undesirable long range effects on the child.

"Except for my aunt's informing me of my father's death, no one talked to me about it", says a young woman whose father died when she was ten. "This silence went on for many years... I still find it hard to utter the words 'father', 'my dad', 'death' in conversation or to write them". The same subject also recounted that for many years she had thought that her father was waiting for someone to come and help him to get out of his grave, and that she ought to do it. It is to be assumed that such painful thoughts could have been prevented if the child had been in a more free and open atmosphere and if she could have talked to someone about what she felt and thought.

Another subject, whose father died when he was 13, also said that he found it difficult to talk about his deceased father. "Despite the fact that we knew he was dying, his death was a shock... At home no one spoke about it... I went through a crisis at school, I had to repeat the year and I was referred to a psychologist as a result of severe headaches that I suffered from."

"What made things the most difficult was the fact that no one spoke of mother," said one subject. "There was this terrible silence that went on for years... I couldn't bring myself to utter the word mother..."

"Everyone was afraid to talk to me about my father," said another subject. "they even refrained from talking about fathers in general so as not to remind me. As a result, when I entered high school I didn't even tell anyone that I had no father. Now I think that it would have been better if I had talked about him."

"The fact that mother never cried in our presence was hard on me," said a young subject who lost his father when he was a teenager. "When she felt the need to cry, she would run to her bedroom, shut the door and cry there. I didn't know what to do. This was the most difficult thing to bear. I felt it as a physical pain."

80

A similar feeling of distress resulting from emotional restraint was described by another subject. "My aunt told me, tearfully, that my mother was dead but I couldn't cry. This bothered me... and then, when my father burst into heart-rending tears I too began crying... My aunt hugged me and the three of us cried together. Aferwards I felt a tremendous relief."

"I don't remember my mother crying, although it is clear to me that she must have cried," said a young subject whose father was killed in an accident when she was eight. "Mother claimed that we must look to the future and forget the past... We must not talk or cry about it."

A more positive feeling, which is evidence of the open approach to death, is expressed by some of the following subjects: "The kibbutz published a booklet in memory of my father, and through this booklet, as well as through talks with my mother, I got to know my father," said a subject whose father was killed in war when she was a baby. "My talks with mother meant a lot to me ... we used to sit for hours and talk about what kind of a person father was and how he died."

"What helped me," said a young subject who had lost his mother, "were my talks with my sister about mother. I felt the need to remember her, to revive her image, to know more about her and her illness..."

One of the subjects told of a tradition practiced by the Ministry of Defense — having a gathering of all the war orphans from time to time: "It's wonderful seeing everybody, talking to them and hearing how they are faring. I correspond with some of them and I see that I'm not the only one having a hard time..."

As has been pointed out, understanding the concepts of finality and irreversibility is critical for the beginning of the mourning process of the child and for his acceptance of death (first phase), but it is also important in the second phase of mourning. Preoccupation with worrying about the deceased (is he feeling pain, is he cold?), i.e., not accepting death's finality, or fantasies about meeting the deceased as a person alive again, and not accepting death's irreversibility, prevent the child from concentrating on his own feelings. He is hindered from focusing on his/her pain and his grief, since he/she is still preoccupied with his/her decease parent's fate. It is important to allow the child to deal with his/her own feelings because working through his/her feelings and their significance is vital at this stage of the mourning process. This phase leads the child toward detachment from the deceased and allows him/her to rebuild his world without him/her.

In addition to deepening understanding of death's finality and its irreversibility, the second phase of mourning requires understanding of two additional concepts, causality and inevitability. At this stage it is important to help the child to understand the objective biological causes of the death in order to diminish his/her tendency to blame himself/herself for the death or to blame the deceased or people in his environment. Although cognitive understanding of the concept of causality does not guarantee prevention of guilt feelings, it is vital to the process of emotional acceptance of the objective causes of the death.

Understanding the concept of inevitability is important towards the end of the second phase of mourning and the beginning of readjustment to a new reality, which does not include the deceased. Recognition of the fact that sooner or later everyone dies may make it easier for the child to overcome his/her doubts and to deal with the crucial question "Why did it have to be my father?" This enables him/her to achieve gradual emotional acceptance of the fact of death and of the inevitable newly-created situation.

A study (see description of this study on page 242) was conducted among elementary school children to establish the connection between a child's being orphaned and his understanding of causality and inevitability. It showed a slight inferiority on the part of orphans in conceptualizing these two aspects of death in comparison to children in the control group, who were the same age and of the same background and intelligence. However, the gap between the two groups was not significant. Especially prominent was the difference between the two groups in their understanding of causality in human death, with orphans scoring significantly lower. In addition, the findings showed that war ophans attending first grade who were from a culturally deprived background scored significantly lower in their understanding of the inevitability of human death than did non-orphans. War orphans from educated families who were attending third grade also scored significantly lower in their understanding of the concepts causality and inevitability than did non-orphans.

2. *Interviews with adults who were orphaned in childhood show the importance of visiting the gravesite.* From the interviews it appears that a visit to the gravesite of a deceased parent is a positive and desirable act in two spheres. It helps the orphan to grasp the fact of death and it satisfies his emotional need to remember and feel close to the deceased.

"It is desirable to take children to the gravesite of their deceased parent immediately after the death, even if they are of a tender age," explained one of the subjects, "they ought to know that this is where their father (or mother) is buried."

"It is very important to visit the gravesite, to see something tangible connected with the deceased," said a subject who lost his mother in childhood and who was not taken to the cemetery until several years later.

"The grave and the tombstone help to make death tangible and therefore children of any age should be taken to visit the gravesite," said a young subject who lost her father when she was six. "However, the child should be prepared in advance for such a visit. The surviving parent and the child should talk about what happened... it is very important that they should cry together at the gravesite."

The last element mentioned, which emphasizes the importance of weeping and expression of feeling at the gravesite, and accepts them as legitimate, is repeated in interviews with other subjects as well: "When I'm in a bad mood, we go to visit the gravesite," said a subject who had lost her father. "When I feel like 'talking' to him, I feel more free to do it there..." Another subject who felt the same way added that she visited her father's graveside for memorial services and "on all significant occasions in my life, such as my wedding day... that sort of makes him a part of what is happening to me..."

In conclusion it can be said, then, that visiting the gravesite is of great importance for the orphaned child, both for the part it plays in making the fact of death more tangible, and as part of a family custom which provides an element of satisfaction of profound emotional needs.

3. *The teacher also has an important role in the phase of working through the mourning.* As stated before, the orphaned child is unable to work through the process of mourning alone. Mourning is a psychosocial process. In dealing with it the child needs help from adults, particularly the adults who are significant in his life. Many orphans find it difficult to talk directly to their teachers about their feelings and their anxieties. This difficulty stems from several factors: Avoidance to talk about pain and grief represents an effort (though an ineffective one) to repress these feelings; The child may not wish to draw attention to his problem by talking about it; he does not want to be different from other children. Nevertheless, it must be remembered that such a child *is* different from other children. He/she has been through a traumatic experience and this must be taken into account. He/she needs help to rebuild the reality of his/her life. Some children are afraid that the teacher may not understand their feelings and therefore refrain from sharing their pain and perplexity.

The role of the teacher at this stage of mourning is therefore mainly to provide support and to encourage the child to talk about the things that preoccupy and trouble him. This must be dealt with both on the cognitive level (difficulty in understanding certain aspects of death, for instance) and on the emotional level (guilt, or missing his parent, for instance). Moreover, the teacher must show understanding and sensitivity for the tremendous grief and pain that the bereaved child is feeling. There should be complete acceptance of him, even when his behavior is strange and non-conformist. The teacher has varied possibilities and opportunities for establishing contact with the child as follows:

1. In reaction to deviant behavior on the child's part, such as an outburst of tears, or significant withdrawal from the other children and into himself.

2. In response to a hint from the child of his willingness to talk about the subject ("my Dad bought me this shirt...") a conversation can be initiated.

3. An occasion, such as memorial day, for instance, can be exploited.

4. A talk about the deceased parent and the orphan's situation can be initiated without any special occasion or pretext.

It must be remembered that although elementary-school-age children have a fairly realistic understanding of the concepts of death, their conceptualization of death is still not mature and there may be gaps in their understanding of the concept. The traumatic experience that the orphan goes through and his/her intense emotional involvement may lead to a distortion in his/her understanding of some of the concepts of death. It is therefore very important to help the child to gain a sound grasp of these concepts, which serve as the basis for emotional working through of the process of mourning.

My Friends Make Me Mad

At first I was spoiled by everyone.
Relatives and neighbors
Forgave me all my pranks.
They showered me with favors,
And bought me balls and tanks.

But why is it that all the kids
And even my best friend
Force me to remember things
And don't seem to understand?

Why, only yesterday, after the game
David spitefully said,
"So what if you won, it's not the same,
Because you don't have no Dad".

It's true I have no father,
But why do they rub it in?
I know I am an orphan
But why is that a sin?

Phase 3: *Adjustment to the new reality*

The third phase of mourning is the phase in which the orphan finds his place in the new reality, which does not include the deceased. At this stage he/she accepts the fact that reality has changed, that his/her deceased parent is no longer a part of it. As he accepts this, he gradually builds up a new self-image. He understands that he is now different from other children in that he has no father (or mother). In all other aspects which make up his self-image, however, he remains as he was. The orphan expects those around him to treat him according to this new self-image. He expects them to take into account the change that has taken place in his world, while also remembering that he is essentially the same person that he was before. At the same time he expects to be treated like other children rather than being pitied or overprotected. In this phase, too, after the bereaved child has detached himself from the deceased and is in the process of rebuilding his world, the help of adults is very important to him.

The orphan is troubled by questions about his new world and his future. Until now his father (or mother) was an almost inseparable part of his actions. From now on he must deal with events and problems by himself or with the help of other people. There are times when others withdraw, overprotect or insult the orphan. Such behavior has adverse effects on the orphan's readjustment to his class and to his new reality. This represents a drastic change for the orphan and arouses many anxieties.

It is important to remember that just as during the previous phase, at this stage of readjustment the orphan will not always initiate talks about his future and about his/her new situation. This may be because he/she does not know to what extent others might wish to share his/her doubts or because he/she is afraid of hurting others – particularly his surviving parent – by speaking about the deceased parent. That is why his teacher is so important, as the person who can encourage the child to express his/her anxieties and fears about how he/she will get along without his/her deceased parent. The teacher should encourage him to be realistic in recognizing his parent's irrevocable departure. At the same time he must be given the feeling that there are people on whom he can depend for building a new framework for his/her life. The teacher's involvement in the matter, the extent to which she accepts the child and his anxieties, and his willingness to talk about the problems are all crucial in determining the amount of confidence the child will show in the adults in his environment as well as his/her willingness to talk about his problems, now and in the future.

Upon learning of the misfortune, the teacher should talk with the children in the class about it and encourage them to express their feelings. Before the orphan returns to school, the teacher should explain the change that has occurred, to the other children, the orphan's present needs should be considered. The other children's sensitivity to his situation will ease the orphan's readjustment to the class. It will give him/her confidence and the feeling that not all his/her world has been destroyed, and that a significant part of the world – his/her class – has remained stable, sympathetic and understanding.

Who Am I Now

Ever since my brother died
People don't treat me the same
As if I'm a different person
And only have the same name.

At school, if I'm late, my teacher
Is never angry with me.
No matter how awful my work is
I never get less than 'B'.

Everyone is very protective
As if I were fragile and slim
They treat me like a baby
And humor my every whim.

Will they never allow me
To be myself again?
Will I ever return to be normal
And one of the gang again?

Part Three

TEACHERS' QUESTIONS AND CHILDREN'S CONVERSATIONS ON THE SUBJECT OF DEATH

As part of his daily work the teacher encounters specific problems connected with orphans, such as their deviant behavior or questions they may ask. Moreover, the teacher hears questions and remarks of non-orphaned children on the subject of death. A child may ask the teacher a direct question on the subject (in response to a certain stimulus, such as a dead bird), or the class may expect the teacher to introduce the subject (on a memorial day, for instance) although this expectation is not expressed. Many teachers have raised questions which express their uncertainty about how to handle children's questions and problems related to death.

It is our assumption that the problems raised by children (orphans and non-orphans) on the subject of death should not be evaded. Children seek answers to their questions. An answer given by an adult whom the child trusts will help him/her to gain a realistic grasp of the circumstance of death and the new reality following it. If the child is not provided with a reliable explanation, he will try to answer the questions himself. In most cases these answers will be childish, unrealistic, imaginary, frightening and distorting. His misconceptions will consequently have adverse effects on his readjustment.

A sample of 220 elementary-school and preschool teachers were asked to take part in a study on this topic. They were asked to record various problems they encountered in their work which were connected with the subject of death and with which they would like help. The questions were many and have been divided according to category, by three independent judges.

Following is a sampling of the questions asked by teachers, − divided into two principal areas:

A. Problems connected with development of the five concepts of death − irreversibility, finality, causality, inevitability and old age.

B. Problems connected with the process of mourning − notification of death, rites of mourning, readjustment of the orphan.

Chapter 1: Teacher's questions and children's conversation about the concept of death's irreversibility

A. Teachers' questions

1. When an orphan asks what becomes of the dead, what should he be told?
2. When an orphan asks whether there is life after death, what should I answer?
3. How should I respond when an orphan says, "I think my dead daddy will come back"?
4. At the end of the school-day an orphan who had lost his mother six months before asked me, "When will my mother come to take me home?"
5. The mother of a first grader asked my advice on how she should have answered him when he asked "Mother, when is daddy going to finish work in dead and come back home?"
6. What should I say to an orphan who said, "Daddy has gone to Europe, hasn't he?"
7. What should I say to an orphan who asks, "Can my daddy see me when he looks down from heaven?"
8. What should I say to an orphan who said, "When I grow up I'm going to be an astronaut and then I can fly high into the sky and meet my mother."
9. How should I react if an orphan comes to me with a distorted explanation which he heard at home: "My mother said that Daddy would come back from heaven soon."

The concept of irreversibility requires acknowledgement of death as an irreversible phenomenon and of our inability to turn back the biological course of life, and relinquishment of the deceased as a living person. The biological process of life ceases with death and this process is absolutely irreversible. The deterioration of the dead body is a process of no return. Only after cognitive understanding of this, can the orphan begin the process of mourning. This is a painful process characterized by difficulty in emotional acceptance of the fact of death and the final severance. At the end of the process the orphan finally accepts what can not be changed on the basis of the proof that reality furnishes. Each day serves as additional proof that the deceased will never return.

When an orphan says, "I think my daddy will come back", he is expressing a wish that he feels throughout the process of mourning, until his final acceptance of death. This wish and the fact that he misses his deceased parent should be met with understanding. At the same time, it must be unequivocally made clear to the child that his/her deceased parent will never return. Actually, in the question on what becomes of the dead, the child was trying to find out whether there is a possibility that his deceased parent will return. Therefore, it is very important to stress that death is a state opposite to life. Death means cessation of life, and therefore the deceased no longer exists as a living person anywhere or in any way. Moreover, there is no possibility of a dead person returning to life. The body eventually deteriorates in its grave and all that is left to us of the deceased, are our memories of him.

The teacher's fear that the harsh truth may hurt the child, particularly the orphaned child, may sometimes lead to a false explanation about what happens to the deceased after death. The teacher may leave the child with the impression that there is some hope that the deceased will return, or he may falsely describe a life after death similar to our real life. In both cases the effort to protect the child from the harsh truth is destructive. Belief in the possibility of the deceased returning some day as a living person prevents the orphan from beginning the mourning process. This process is vital to his detachment from the deceased and to the devotion of his emotional energy to new objects.

In all that a child says about life after death, he is expressing his wish to be reunited with his father as a living person. It is important not to delude the child, not to give him false hope, but instead, to help him face reality, with all the pain and grief involved. There is no chance of the child's seeing his deceased parent again. That must be made clear to the orphan as well as to non-orphans. Any effort on the teacher's part to mitigate the severity of objective truth in order to make things easier for the child, may eventually have the disastrous results of the orphan's being unable to accept the new reality. He/she continues to live in expectation of a reunion with his deceased parent as a living person. Such an expectation robs the child of most of his energy so that he/she is too preoccupied to deal with the everyday realities of his life.

Teachers often encounter the problem of erroneous information being given the orphan by members of his family, as in the case of a child whose mother told him that his father would return from heaven. This problem is particularly difficult because the teacher will not wish to undermine the surviving parent's credibility. Despite the important role that the surviving parent plays in the mourning process of his children, he/she is often unsure of how to behave with them and of how to answer their questions, since he/she has had no previous experience of such a painful situation. Moreover, he/she is not always able, at this stage, to give the orphans all the attention they need since he/she has himself/herself undergone a traumatic experience and is absorbed in himself and his own pain. In many cases the parent needs advice and guidance by someone who is aware of the needs of the orphan during the process of mourning.

When the teacher encounters the problem of a child being misinformed by his family, he cannot and must not ignore it, despite his fear of undermining the parent's credibility. The teacher, recognizing the destructive effect that such misinformation will have on the child, must tell the child the truth, while showing understanding for what the parent wishes the truth to be. It is important for him to have a talk with the parent and explain how important the child's having a sound understanding of the concepts of death is for his ability to mourn and readjust.

B. **Conversations among children or between children and adults on the subject**

1. – Dalit (a 3.5-year old girl): Yoav's dog was run over, so Yoav will now make a miracle and the dog will come back to life.
    – Yoram (5): No, he won't. If the dog has been buried, he can't come back to life. Dead is dead forever.

— Gadi (7): His heart has stopped working and so has his brain. If his brain has stopped working, he can never be alive again. Even if he hasn't been buried, he won't ever be alive again.

This conversation illustrates the development in the understanding of the concept of irreversibility between the ages of 3 1/2 and 7.

2. — Amir (6, after hearing from his mother that an uncle had died): Mother, will uncle Jacob never return home?
   — Mother: No, he won't. He's dead.
   — Amir: What will they do to him?
   — Mother: He will be buried in the ground, and we will be able to see him only in pictures and remember how he used to play with you. We'll also be able to go and put flowers on his grave.

3. The father of Miri, 7, has been killed in an accident and her mother is telling her about it.
   — Miri: Where's father?
   — Mother: Father has gone away, for a very long time.
   — Miri: He has a lot of work to do there. He'll be away for a very long time.

The difference between the two previous examples must be noted. In the case of Amir, his mother was less emotionally involved in the death of his uncle and was therefore better able to explain the irreversibility of death. In the case of Miri, although she was a year older than Amir, her mother was unable to tell her the truth, because of her greater emotional involvement and her own pain.

4. The teacher is telling a first grade class that Ronit's father has died.
   — Children: Then she will never see him again?
   — Teacher: No, because he's dead. The dead never return to life.
   — Children: What happens to them?
   — Teacher: The deceased is no longer a person. He is buried and covered over with ground. Ronit will never see him again. She will be able to look at his pictures and remember how he used to play with her.

Children find it hard to accept that the dead will never be seen again. They need a concrete explanation of what happens to the deceased. He/she being buried makes it easier for them to accept death's irreversibility on the cognitive level.

When Will My Father Return

I keep asking my mother,
"When is Dad coming back?"
I won't take no for an answer,
Why doesn't Dad come back?

I want to see him just once more,
I want him to take my hand,
And tell me just like he used to
That I'm his good little friend.

And I stubbornly wait at the station
For him to come, just on vacation...

Chapter 2: Teachers' questions and children's conversations about the concept of death's finality

A. Teachers' questions about the Concept of Finality

1. What shall I say to a child who asks what happens to the body in the grave?
2. What shall I say to an orphan who asks, "Does daddy feel that he is dead?"
3. When some white mice we had in the animal corner in the classroom died, the children asked if it hurts to die.
4. On a rainy day an orphan came up to me and said, "My mother is probably feeling very cold in her grave now." How should I have reacted?
5. An orphan said to me, "Isn't it awful that the worms are eating my father now?" How should I have reacted?
6. After having visited his father's gravesite in the company of his grandmother, an orphan told me that his grandmother cried very loudly because his father was in the grave and he couldn't hear her if she cried softly. How should I have reacted?

Understanding the finality of death involves understanding that death is the termination of all the processes of life, whether seen or unseen. All biological functions which characterize life, such as functioning of the inner organs, sensation, thought and consciousness, cease to exist in the dead. The deceased is not a person in any sense that characterizes life. Recognition of the fact of death's finality is no doubt difficult, for children as well as for adults. Many teachers wonder if they aren't hurting the child by making it clear to him that death is final and that the body undergoes a process of deterioration after it is buried.

The question is whether by hiding the truth or blurring it we are helping the orphan to adjust to his new situation. Understanding death's finality is important at all stages of mourning. When the child's subjective conceptualization coincides with the factual situation, and when he/she understands that death means the severance of all physical ties between the orphan and his/her deceased parent, he/she can begin the process of mourning. At its end he/she will reach emotional acceptance of the fact of physical severance, of separation from his/her parent, and of readjustment to a reality which does not include the deceased parent.

From the questions raised by the teachers it is clear that bereaved children may be preoccupied by thoughts of what happens to the body in the grave. To the orphan, the grave is the new 'home' of his deceased parent because he was buried there. The orphan seeks reassurance that his parent feels good in his new 'home', that he/she is not lonely, or cold, or in pain. These fears preoccupy and trouble the orphan and arouse painful feelings and anxieties. These anxieties can be relieved by making it clear to the bereaved child that death is a final state in which all the processes of life stop, so that the deceased can no longer feel anything, biologically. He/she feels no pain, cold, or hunger. He/she does not see or hear. At the same time, the bereaved child must be made to feel that his teacher understands his/her feelings and anxieties, that he/she understands that he/she misses the deceased, that he/she is willing to listen to his/her questions and try to help him/her solve his/her problems.

It is not desirable to try to gloss over the facts and reassure the child by saying that the grave is well sealed, that the body is in a closed coffin which protects it from the cold, etc. This will not diminish the child's fears and anxieties, since the only way to do this is to deny the possibility of a body being able to feel at all. Unless the child understands that a body can not feel anything, his/her imagination will always invent new situations which arouse anxiety.

An adult must help the child towards cognitive acceptance of the fact that death means the cessation of all the processes of life, and that the grave is not meant to preserve the body. Deterioration and disintegration are part of the process that the body must undergo, but this process takes place when the deceased no longer feels it. Accepting death's finality will free the child from worrying about his deceased parent. It will enable him/her to concentrate on his/her feelings, his/her pain, his/her detachment from the deceased parent, and his/her adjustment to a new reality.

When People Die

The body is motionless,
All life has left it.
The heart no longer beats,
The lungs no longer breathe,
It has no voice,
It makes no noise,
All life has left it.

The body is at rest,
Peaceful, quiet rest.
It hears no rain
It feels no pain
The dead feel no distress.

B. Children's Conversations about the Concept of Finality

1.   – Itay (4, to Lior, 4 1/2, finishing a story): "So at night the dead man will come out of his grave and visit people's houses and take all the bad children away."
   – Mother: "Itay, it's not nice to tell such stories."
   – Ronit (8): "It's not true at all. The dead can't leave their grave because they can't move. They aren't people any more, they're just dead."

There is an essential difference between the two answers in what they contributed to Itay's understanding of death's finality. The mother's attitude appears to be 'educational', but her remark did nothing to help him overcome his fears. It did not improve his understanding of death's finality. Ronit, on the other hand, corrected his erroneous version of the story and helped him to understand that the dead no longer exist or function as living beings and that they can't leave their grave for the simple reason that they can not move.

2.   – Mother (speaking to a psychologist about her orphaned son): "My son asked me whether his father could still hear and see and when I asked him why he was asking he said,

'Well, because we go to the cemetery, put flowers on his grave, and talk about him. If he can't hear or see, what are we doing it for?' "

— Psychologist: Your child understands that the dead neither hear nor see, but the customs observed in connection with the dead seem to contradict what he knows. It is important that you explain to him that eulogies and putting flowers on the grave are customs to help the living. Talking about the deceased and putting flowers on his grave make his family feel better by helping them to remember him.

3. — A first grader, answering a series of questions on the subject:

— "Does a dead person see? No, because his eyes are shut. Does a dead person move? No, because he's lying down and he can't move.

Can a dead person leave his grave? No, because the grave is made of stone."

Despite the fact that this child knows that a dead person no longer functions, he doesn't understand the significance of death's finality. In his explanation he attributes death's finality to external, technical causes (such as a stone or shut eyes). He does not however, show understanding of the biological process on which death's finality rests.

— A fifth grader, answering the same questions,

"A dead person is no longer alive, so he can't do any of the things that a living person can do. He can't see, or hear, or move."

Some children have to be helped to grasp the significance of death's finality. They have to be helped to understand that death means cessation of all biological functions of the body and that cessation is the cause of the dead body's inability to function as a living being.

The Dead Are No Longer People

I know that the dead are not people,
They do not feel, they do not breathe,
They have no wishes, wants, or needs,
They do not feel, they do not grieve,

And their grave they cannot leave,
They stay in it forever,
They can not come back, ever.

I know that the dead are not living people,
But when it rains or when it snows
My heart to grandpa out it goes
For he is lying in the ground,
And maybe he can hear the sound
Of a downpour and the thunder,
Perhaps he feels the damp down under
Maybe he will get the gout,
Maybe he's trying to get out...

Such thoughts disturb me, but I know
That he can't really hear the snow
He's dead, he cannot feel or see
And those fears sometimes trouble me.
But he lies in his grave peacefully,
He is not calling out to me.

Because the dead are not living people...they are
dead.

Chapter 3: Teachers' questions and children's conversation on the subject of death's causality

A. Teachers' Questions about the Concept of Causality

1. How should I answer an orphan who asks why his father died?
2. How should I react when an orphan says, "I hate my father because he's left us"?
3. A child who was recently orphaned remarked, "My mother died because of me". I didn't know how to react.
4. In my class there is a child whose father died of a heart attack. The child blames himself for his father's death because he didn't get help in time. What should I do?

Understanding the causality of death involves understanding the objective biological causes which led to the parent's death, such as illness, war, old age, etc. It is important to help the child to understand these causes in order to limit, as far as possible, his tendency to blame himself for the death, or to blame the deceased, or other people. This tendency originates from childish thinking, which attributes magical powers to words, thoughts and wishes, and sees them as the causes of events. Thus, a child might take his/her father's/mother's death to be the result of anger and hostility that he/she felt towards his father/mother, or a punishment for his/her own behavior, or his father's/mother's behavior, or for the behavior of other people. Such an interpretation of the cause of death might lead the child to develop severe feelings of guilt, or anger at the deceased for leaving him. He might blame the people around him for the death. Understanding the real causes of death will make it easier for the child to accept himself in his new reality. He will learn to accept the surviving parent, and to complete the process of mourning and detachment from the deceased parent.

The teacher can play an important role in helping the child to understand the concept of causality. In many cases the child is afraid to express his/her anger or his/her guilt in front of the surviving parent. He may find it easier to express these feelings to another adult who plays a significant part in his life, and who is not directly involved in his parent's death. The teacher is such a person. It is therefore important that the teacher should not ignore the orphan's doubts on this subject. He/she must deal with the child's direct questions, even if they are sometimes unexpected and surprising. The teacher should also be sensitive to various signs which indicate that the child has a subjective understanding of the causes of his parent's death and he should react to them. If the orphan provides no opportunity for clarifying the subject, the teacher should initiate a talk on the subject. The orphan must understand the cause of his parent's death, whether he has asked about it or not. It is important to describe the circumstances and the biological causes that led to the death. Only when he has a picture of the circumstances of the death, will the orphan be able to understand the concept of causality on a cognitive level. Such an understanding is not, in itself, a guarantee against anger or guilt. It is, however, essential for the beginning of the process of acceptance of the objective causes for the death.

In saying "I hate my father because he has left us" the orphan is expressing his anger at this father for leaving him to his grief and his pain without the help and support of his father to which he was accustomed. The orphan is also angry with his father because by dying he has made him different from other children. He has left him alone with his worries and anxieties about the future. Despite any initial reservations that the teacher may have about allowing the child to speak in this manner about the deceased parent, it is important to allow the child to express his/her rage, to talk about it, and to understand the reasons behind it. At the same time, the teacher must point out that no one chooses to die and that the deceased parent surely didn't want to die and would have preferred to stay alive and be with his/her family.

"Father died because of me" expresses magical thinking and is typical of the cognitive development of children, particularly in the first grades of elementary school. At this age children believe that death is a punishment for the behavior of certain people or the result of wishes that are realized by means of certain people or the result of wishes that are realized by means of the child's 'omnipotent' powers. It is important to make it clear to the orphan, as well as to all the children in the class, that a parent's death in no way depends on his child's thoughts or behavior and is not affected by them at all. Sometimes, however, there are objective circumstances connected with the parent's death which make it possible for the responsibility for the death to be laid on one particular member of the family. If, for instance, a man is killed in an accident after having had an argument with someone in his family, it can be presumed that if he hadn't been angry he would have concentrated more on his driving and would not have been killed. It is important, therefore, to understand why an orphan is feeling guilty for the death of his/her parent. The teacher should talk to the child about the painful feelings accompanying guilt and try to help him/her gain a better perspective of objective reality and the objective causes that led to his/her parent's death.

B. Children's conversations about the concept of causality

1. A group of children is responding to a poem by Yonatan Gefen.
   - Dana (3 1/2): Anat's mother died because Anat was a bad girl (i.e. moral cause — death as a punishment of Anat).
   - Miri (4 1/2): She died because she was sick and they couldn't save her, or maybe the police killed her because she was bad (i.e. a mixture of biological and moral causes for the death).
   - Gila (5 1/2): Anat's mother died because she was old, or because she caught a cold (i.e. clearcut biological cause).

From these children's responses we clearly see the progressive development of the concept of causality with age. Initially, a moral cause is provided for death, then there is a mixture of moral and biological causes, and finally only biological causes are seen.

2. - Shalom (7, to his teacher, after seeing a dead dog): What do dogs die of?
   - Teacher: Just like human begins, dogs die of old age, or because they are ill.
   - Shalom: Can a dog grow old?
   - Teacher: Yes, but it's harder to tell when a dog is old.

Only people who know the dog well can tell that he is growing old.

The teacher's answer helped Shalom to clarify his concept of causality of death. The teacher correctly pointed out that both people and dogs die, and of similar causes, and that dogs die of old age too though the signs of old age are more difficult to distunguish in animals.

3. — Yoram (7, an orphan, answering the question 'What do people die of?'): When a boy has been bad, can he die as a punishment?

This example clearly shows the connection between guilt and the attribution of death to moral causes. This orphan was feeling guilty and as a result his self-image was low. He felt he was a 'bad boy' and reasoned that to be 'bad' was a sufficient cause for punishment by death. Although the teacher can do a lot to help in such cases, it might be well to refer children who suffer from such guilt to a psychologist or psychiatrist.

Why

Please answer me, why,
Oh, answer me why,
Why did my father
Have to die?

Why did my mother let him go?
Why couldn't she have said 'No'
Why did she let him go off to war,
To the fire and thunder it held in store,
Why couldn't she have locked the door?
And now we won't see him forevermore.

And I,
Why was I silent when he said goodbye?
But he seemed to understand,
When I just held on to Mother's hand,
And his voice was hoarse when he took the other
And said, 'Be a good boy, and help your mother.'
Then he kissed us and left.
Oh, why did it have to be my father?

Chapter 4: Teachers' Questions and Children's Conversations on the Concepts of Death's Inevitability and Old Age

A. Teachers' questions abut the concept of Inevitability

1. One of the children asked me, "Haya, are you going to die, too?"
2. When Yossi's father died, one of the children remarked, "Yossi's father died. Is my father going to die, too?"
3. One of the children in my class said, "My grandfather is old but he's never going to die; no one in our family dies." How should I have reacted?

Understanding the inevitability of death involves understanding that death is an unavoidable phenomenon, irregardless of the cause of death. That means understanding that all life must end in death, death being part of the biological sequence of life.

Children in the first grades of elementary school (particularly first grade), though they show a certain understanding of old age as a cause of death, still tend to exclude themselves and those close to them from the category of 'those who die'.

Understanding the fact that all human beings must eventually die arouses anxiety in children, and the fear that they might soon lose those near and dear to them. In orphans, this anxiety is accompanied by a certain relief. The question 'why did it have to be my father?" loses some of its poignancy when the orphan recognizes death's inevitability. If death is inevitable, then his father/mother would have had to die sooner or later, just like everyone must. Only certain circumstances caused him/her to die sooner. Understanding the concept of inevitability enables the orphan to accept himself/herself in his/her new situation and diminishes his/her sense of being different, putting this difference in the correct perspective.

The sentence "My grandfather is old but he's never going to die; no one in our family dies", reflects the thinking of a first grader that death does not come to all peple. Six and seven year-olds doubt that their parents will die someday and that the same fate awaits them, too. Even when a child of this age recognizes old age as part of the cycle of life, he/she still does not make the connection between that and the inevitability of death when it comes to himself and to those close to him/her.

It is important to make it clear to children that death may be the result of a variety of causes and that it is inevitable. Understanding that all human beings must die will help the child to accept the death of people in his/her environment as part of a biological process which applies to all human beings, rather than to a special phenomenon which might have been avoided. Such questions as "Haya, are you going to die too?" and "Is my father going to die too?" reveal a basic understanding of the concept that death is inevitable along with anxiety and fear of the possibility that people close to the child may die.

Many adults tend to try and minimize such a possibility, wishing to spare the child anxiety. It is important to understand that anxiety associated with death exists in any case and denying death's inevitability will not prevent such anxiety. The anxiety and its causes should be brought out into the open and discussed, and it should be pointed out to the child that most people die when they are old and that their old age is a long way off.

B. **Children's conversations about the Concept of Inevitability and old age**

1. – Nahum (6): I will never die.
   – Ettie (7): Of course you'll die, when you're old. You may die before that in war, and then you won't grow old.

Nahum is only one year younger than Ettie, but his conceptualization of death is much poorer than Ettie's. His anxiety about death causes him to deny the universality of old age and death.

2. – Adi (6): Do all old people die?
   – Mother: Yes, they all die.
   – Adi: Then why isn't grandfather dead?
   – Mother: He isn't very old yet, and he is very healthy.
   – Adi: Then I won't die either, because I'm not sick.

Adi is excluding herself from the category of people who must die by hanging a false conclusion on one random word of her mother's.

She reasons that if her grandfather is old and hasn't died because he's healthy, then she herself, who is both young and healthy, certainly won't die. Adi's mother did not pursue this conversation further, perhaps because she didn't know what to say. It would have been well for her to say something like, "That's right, you're still young and healthy, but all people, when they get very old, die." At this point Adi might become anxious and ask, "Will my grandfather die, then?" Here mother might answer, "All people die. We hope, though, that grandfather will be with us for a long while yet." In such an answer the mother would be telling her child the truth but at the same time responding to her emotional need for reassurance.

    3.   This conversation took place in a kibbutz.

         — Tamar (6): Is your dog sick? How come he doesn't move?
         — Yoav (4): Mother says he's only old.
         — Tamar: Then he's going to die soon.
         — Yoav: No, he isn't. Dogs can be old all their lives and not die.
         — Tamar (emphatically): All old dogs eventually die, when it's too late to save them.

Yoav is making an effort to exclude his dog, to whom he is apparently attached, from the inevitability of death. Tamar, being older and not emotionally involved in the matter, shows much better conceptualization of old age and the inevitability of death.

    4.   — Danny (an 8-year-old whose father was killed in war): Why was my Daddy killed? All the other Daddies are returning from the war, so why did my Daddy die?
         — Mother: You know that your Daddy was killed when his tank was hit by a bomb. There were many tanks that weren't hit.

Danny is asking the eternal Jobian question, which distresses all the bereaved — Why of all people, my father? — Danny's mother uses causality to answer his question. Danny already knows how his father was killed. So that he may accept the inevitability of death, it is necessary to explain to Danny that his father died now, but all fathers must eventually die, because all people must die.

    5.   — Yoav (a six-year-old orphan, whose father was killed in war): Why did it have to be my father that was killed?

There were many soldiers in tanks so why did the bomb have to fall on him? Couldn't he have run away?

Yoav's pain might be somewhat relieved by an explanation emphasizing the inevitability of death and the range of its causes, including old age. In answer his mother could have said something like, "It's true that your father died in war, but in the end no one can avoid death. No óne can avoid old age."

6. — Lior (9, to his teacher, after a visit to the cemetery): You have no idea how many soldiers are buried at the cemetery. Teacher: Yes, Lior, your father was not the only one killed in the war. There are many bereaved families, just like yours. There are also children whose fathers died but not in war and they all must be equally sad.

At the cemetery Lior realized that he was not the only one in his situation. His teacher stressed that death is a universal phenomenon and that sooner or later everyone is touched by it.

Secrets

It's true, I'm only a child,
I'm only eight years old,
But even children know about
Which secrets aren't told.

The secrets that we keep from others,
And never, never tell our mothers
Are of things like cutting class,
Misbehaving, breaking glass,
Pulling braids, planning raids,
Stealing bikes, and the likes.

But why is no one telling me why,
Why my daddy had to die?
He went off to war and never came back
And now they're whispering behind my back
Speaking among themselves secretly,
Keeping things from me and shaming me.

I want to know, I have the right,
What happened when Dad went off to fight
I want to know where, how, and why he died.

107

Chapter 5: Teachers' Questions Concerning the Process of Mourning

A. Teachers' questions about notification of death

Being notified of his parent's death is a critical stage in the orphan's process of mourning. Many teachers raised questions concerning the significance of the act of notification and about the teacher's role at this stage. The reason behind the many questions on this subject lies in the fact that the school is often actively involved in notifying the child: A relative may come to school and notify the teacher of the tragedy. He/she may come to the classroom to take the child home so that the surviving parent may tell him/her of the death, or the teacher may be asked to notify the child. Sometimes the teacher may even encounter a case in which the child returns to school not having been told of his parent's death or having been misled about it.

Following is a sample of teachers' questions:

1. Beginning with what age should a child be told about his parent's death?
2. What should children aged 4-10 be told about a parent's death? Are they old enough to understand what death is?
3. Shouldn't the notification of the child be put off as long as possible?
4. Isn't it better, in the case of very young children, to convey the information about the tragedy in stages? The child can first be told that his parent is ill and after a while, that his parent has died.
5. Who should be the one to tell the child?
6. Should the teacher be the one to tell a child about his parent's death?

The question whether it is desirable for the child to know about his parent's death is the key to the understanding of the process of mourning and readjustment that the orphan must experience. With the parent's death a change occurs in the child's objective reality. Therefore he/she must acknowledge the death — on the cognitive as well as on the emotional level — before he/she can rebuild his world.

His world will no longer include the deceased parent, except as a memory. Without the clear and unequivocal knowledge that the parent is dead and that he will never see him/her again (and this knowledge is at the basis of the child's cognitive understanding of the fact of death), the orphan can not begin the process of mourning. During the mourning process be gains emotional acceptance of the fact of death, of his/her being forever parted from his/her parent, and of his/her readjustment to a new reality. That is to say, the child must know of his parent's death before he/she can go through a sound mourning at the end of which he/she will be able to readjust.

In notifying a child of his parent's death, his/her age and cognitive level must be taken into consideration. It is incorrect to assume that a child of kindergarten age is too young to understand what death is. The findings of a study with Israeli children show that even at pre-kindergarten age children have some initial understanding of concepts related to death. However, since at this age a child thinks in concrete rather than in abstract terms, the explanation given him of the significance of death should be suited to his/her level of thinking and should be specific and clear.

Israeli first graders' conceptualization of irreversibility and finality is fairly well developed and only a few children of this age fail to understand that finality includes cessation of sensation. At this age children begin explaining death in biological terms such as 'You die when your heart stops beating'. The concept of inevitability, too, becomes clearer, though many children still fail to make the connection between old age and inevitability of death. They thus exclude themselves and those close to them from the category of people who die. Despite progress made at this age in the understanding of causality, many children still don't name old age as a cause of death. Thus, from first grade on, a child already possesses a fairly well-based understanding of the concept of death, and is not too young to deal with the subject.

It is important to explain to a child in detail, and in terms he can understand, the various elements that are included in the concept of death and the significance of each of these elements for him. Delaying notification of death, or notifying a child in stages may have adverse consequences. Credibility is crucial for the beginning of a proper mourning process at the proper time. This is true both for adults and children. However, it is even more important for children due to the fact that they are at an age when the difference between reality and imagination is not yet clearly distinguished. The adult is an important representative of the 'real truth'. If at the initial stage of the tragedy some things are kept from the child (even if this is done with good intentions) it will be difficult for him later to believe things that adults tell him, whether they are related to the truth about his parent's death or whether they are explanations of the concepts of death. The fact that adults have changed the version of the truth they told once ("Daddy is in hospital", "Daddy's gone to Europe"), prevents the child from believing any version they may later tell. Why should he believe the very fact of his parent's death, a fact which is so difficult and painful for him to accept, if he discovers a gap in the credibility of the adults who told him about it? Who can guarantee that any additional information given him by adults about his parent's death or about death in general is to be believed? It is therefore important to notify the child of his/her parent's death as soon as possible and not to conceal or change any details in an effort to 'protect' the child.

The question of who should notify the child of his/her parent's death is connected to the question of how the child should be notified. Any adult who is close enough to the child to be trusted by him/her and who is aware of, and sensitive to the special needs of the child in this painful situation can notify the child. The adult notifying the child needs empathy and sensitivity to the child's pain together with an awareness of the importance of the credibility, reliability and accuracy of the information he/she is imparting.

The tendency to think that the surviving parent should be the one to notify the child has not been justified by facts. The surviving parent is often in such a bad emotional state that he/she may be unable to respond to the child's needs at this time.

There is no doubt that the child can also be notified by his/her teacher. As has been pointed out, the teacher is a significant person in the child's life. The teacher often knows the child better than do other adults in his environment, and therefore is better able to notify the child in an atmosphere of empathy and in a manner which will arouse his trust and belief. Moreover, by means of the act of notification the teacher shares in the child's difficult experience. This involvement of the teacher will later make it easier for the child to return to school, because he will know that 'the class knows'. This will serve as the basis for the child's involving the teacher in any problem connected with his parent's death which may arise in the future.

B. Teachers' questions Connected with the Orphan's Participation in Rites of Mourning

Many researchers stress the importance of rites of mourning as a social mechanism which helps the individual to deal with death and bereavement. The existence of long-established customs of mourning makes it easier for the mourner to go through the mourning process and serves to satisfy the emotional needs of the relatives of the deceased. A historical-anthropological survey shows that most ancient myths are evidence of the fact that from the early beginnings of Man's culture he has sought the way to the tree of life. When he did not find it, he evolved complicated and complex ceremonies of disposing of his dead. The customs of burial and mourning form a considerable part of the traditions of most peoples, religions and ethnic groups.

In Israeli Jewish society, beyond the specific customs of each of the ethnic communities there are two prominent customs accepted by all: The funeral and the Shiv'a. These customs serve to illustrate clearly and unequivocally that the mourners are never again to see the deceased. The deceased no longer exists as a living person. His family cannot ignore or deny the fact of his death when so many people join them in mourning the deceased (which also gives the mourning family a feeling of sharing and support).

The grave serves to help the mourner to grasp mentally, and to a certain extent to begin to accept emotionally, the finality of death. It constitutes proof and confirmation of the fact that the deceased has passed away from our world and will remain only in our memory. At the sight of the other graves at the cemetery, the irreversibility of

111

death as well as its universality gradually penetrate the consciousness. This consciousness helps, to a certain extent, in the emotional acceptance of death.

Despite the fact that the funeral and the Shiv'a are two customs practiced and accepted by most Jews, there is still hesitation among adults as to what extent to involve children in these ceremonies, because of the fear that it might do them harm. This hesitation is expressed in the *questions asked by teachers:*

1. Should a child in second or third grade be allowed to attend his parent's funeral?
2. A mother has asked my advice on what she should tell her child, who did not attend his father's funeral, about the funeral.
3. Should I attend the funeral of the parent of a child in my class?
4. The day after his mother's funeral one of the children came to school and caused a stir among the children. In my opinion he should have stayed home all seven days of the Shiv'a. Am I right?
5. Should I visit a child during the Shiv'a, and if his mother hasn't told him about the death or if they just don't mention the deceased at home, what should I talk to the child about?
6. Should I take some of the children in my class to visit the orphan during the Shiv'a?

For children, just as for adults, mourning ceremonies have a therapeutic value. They are important in the orphan's adjustment to the new reality which does not include the deceased parent. This must be explained by teachers to parents, so that they will know how to behave with their children during the critical time following the tragedy.

Grasping the significance of death and of its finality is especially difficult for children. Seeing the grave constitutes one of the first and most basic steps on the way to such understanding. The child's participation in the funeral actualizes the finality of death for him/her. This substantiation is particularly important for children in their concrete phase of thought. The child should see for himself/herself the act of his/her parent being buried in the ground. Although it involves great pain and grief, this act leaves no opening for doubts or imaginings of his parent having gone away or of the grave being some kind of alternate home where the deceased continue to live. During the funeral the child is forced to confront reality and as a result of this he/she cognitively accepts the fact of his/her parent's death. The crying and expression of grief at the funeral also serve to substantiate to the child that a significant and basic change has taken place in his life and that he/she must accept this change.

In the event that the child has not attended the funeral, it is important to provide him with details about the body being buried in the ground. It is also important to take him/her to visit the grave. Such a visit serves to help the child to understand the finality of death and dispels possible fears and fantasies. The child sees that the cemetery is not a new home where his/her deceased parent now lives, but neither is it some horrifying house of phantoms. Visiting the gravesite may contribute to the child's feeling of belonging, which is so important to children. The child feels that he/she is not really all that different from other children, because he too had both parents in the past. The grave serves as proof that the deceased parent did exist in the past as a living person. This is particularly significant for children who never knew the deceased parent. The sight of the many graves surrounding the parent's grave emphasizes the fact that many others have lost their parents too. This makes the child feel less lonely and different.

The seven days of mourning serve to help the widow/widower and the orphans concentrate on the image of the deceased and hold communion with him and the memories associated with him. Everyday life cannot return to normal until the new reality has been grasped and understood and until emotional cognizance has been taken of the new facts. The custom of Shiv'a gathers the family together in its home and makes it possible for friends and neighbors to call on them, to share their mourning, and to help the widow/widower and orphans work out their feeling by talking about and remembering the deceased. All this helps them to accept the fact of death. The weeping and comforting legitimize the expression of feelings. This prevents repression and evasion of an intellectual as well as emotional confrontation of the new situation.

The question arises whether it is desirable that children should stay home all the days of the Shiv'a or whether they should be returned to their daily routine as soon as possible. There is the desire to ease the child's pain by returning him/her as soon as possible to his/her former routine. On the other hand, there is the feeling that the child is part of the family tragedy and that it has important implications for him/her as well.

What Do Grownups Want

What do grownups want of me?
What do they expect to see?

When I with the mourners sit,
And listen to them for a bit,
They quickly chase me out and say,
Why don't you go outside and play?

But when I'm outside with my ball
The neighbors will begin to call
How can you kick a ball around,
And your father buried in the ground?
Have you no shame? At such a time?
As if to play ball is a crime.

And when I sit down in a corner
And turn the pages of a book
I am sure to hear some mourner
Whisper, "He has forgotten him, just look!"

Why don't they understand? Oh, Gee,
What do they expect of me?

It is preferable for the child to stay home with his surviving parent during the seven days of mourning for a number of reasons:
— As a result of his parent's death the child develops a profound sense of loss and bereavement. The significance of his parents for the child and the importance of the emotional bond between them are unquestionably recognized. With the sudden loss of one parent, the child's world is destroyed. He/she now develops anxiety

114

in connection with the surviving parent. He/she is afraid he/she might lose the remaining parent, just as he/she lost the deceased parent. Physical proximity to the surviving parent in the days following the tragedy gives the child a feeling of security and diminishes his/her fears.

The child's presence during the Shiv'a enables him to feel close to the other members of his family and to participate in the conversation about his/her deceased parent and reminisce about him. It legitimizes the expression of various feelings and of his/her sense of weakness and helplessness. It gives him the sense of partnership and empathy which he, like any mourner, needs so much.

-- The child's staying home and away from his normal routine helps him to feel that reality has changed for him and it will never be quite the same.

— The child's staying home makes others in his environment aware of his tragedy and legitimizes his feeling 'different'. He is expected to act differently and express his/her grief and pain in some way, whether these expectations are conveyed to him/her directly or indirectly.

— On the other hand, if the child returns to school before the Shiv'a is over, he/she not only misses participating in the mourning at home, but he may also encounter reactions of amazement or even ridicule on the part of some of his/her clasmates, such as, 'He/she doesn't care about his/her father' or 'He/she has already forgotten', etc. Clearly, the orphan must be spared such an encounter. Criticism makes things more difficult both for the orphan and for the surviving parent, who are suffering the shock of loss.

Leaving the decision of whether to stay home or return to school to the child puts him/her under great pressure and confronts him with a conflict. On one hand he needs to stay close to his/her surviving parent and to be in touch with his pain and with the memory of his/her deceased parent. He needs to deviate from his/her established routine and to how to the pressure of what is expected of him. On the other hand he/she wants to continue his routine of the past, and to deny the fact of death. It is therefore the task of the adults of his/her family to help him to begin the process of mourning immediately following the tragedy and, for this purpose, to encourage him/her to remain home during the Shiv'a with the other members of his family. It is important to note, however, that the child's remaining at home does not mean that he/she is expected to do nothing but talk about his/her deceased parent and his/her tragedy, cry and express his grief, and refrain from any of the daily activities to which he is used. The fact that he/she is not attending school, participating in visits of relatives, friends, neighbors and observing certain customs of mourning in themselves create an atmosphere of mourning in the home and a daily routine that is different. Such activities as playing with a friend, reading a book or watching television reflect the child's effort to keep in touch with ordinary activities in order to relieve his/her pain and to assure himself that many things he/she knew in the past still continue to exist. It assures him that not all in his/her world has been destroyed.

Many teachers are unsure to what extent they should participate in the funeral and the Shiv'a. As pointed out in chapter two, one of the main problems which troubles the orphan following the tragedy is how he/she will return to school, whether his classmates know, and how his/her teachers and classmates will treat him. Will they pity or mock him?

Such questions trouble the orphan and take up much of his emotional energy at a time when he/she needs this energy to accept the fact of death. Many orphans resolve these questions by withdrawing into themselves. When they return to school they are unwilling to share their grief and problems with their teacher or their classmates.

The teacher's participation in the funeral makes him/her a partner in a difficult experience, a painful and central experience in the orphan's life. It paves the way for an attitude of trust, and the child's willingness to share problems connected with the tragedy with his/her teacher. The fact that his/her teacher was present at the funeral, that he/she saw the family in their grief, that he/she shared the child's grief, helps the orphan in the future to share his/her problems with the teacher.

During the Shiv'a various people call on the bereaved family to comfort them, to pray, to reminisce about the deceased, to sympathize and identify. It is important that all this be directed not only to the adult mourners but also to the children. A visit by the teacher and his/her classmates during the Shiv'a is therefore very significant for the orphan. It means that his/her plight is not a secret and that others share his grief and want to comfort him/her and to help him/her come through this difficult time. Such a visit also serves to diminish the child's anxiety in connection with his returning to school.

As to the teacher's hesitation whether, and to what extent, to talk to a child about his/her deceased parent: it has already been pointed out that the family does not always know how to behave with the orphan and how much to tell him/her or what to talk to him/her about. In this sense, as an educator, the teacher represents an authority who can serve as example and guide. The fact that the teacher has brought up the subject will serve as legitimization of conversation about the tragedy, about the child's feelings and about the readjustment he/she will have to make.

Although it is clear that a visit by classmates is beneficial for the orphan, many teachers wonder if it might not be harmful to the other children. Chapter one discussed the importance of preventive aid on the subject of death to children who are not orphans. A visit to a mourning family presents a good opportunity for a "limited mourning" experience. It is a good opportunity for the teacher to talk to the class about death. The children's ability to understand the explanations will be unimpaired, since they are not deeply emotionally involved. It is like a vaccine, which gives the body a light dose of an illness thus strengthening it against the illness in future. Such an experience serves as a 'light dose' of mourning, preparing the child to deal more effectively with more serious cases of future mourning.

After My Brother's Death

They talk about him night and day
They praise his courage, and his deeds.
He was a hero, so they say.
Of me they take no heed.

Since he died, our home
Has been a house of pain and grief.

My parents think of him alone,
And of his life, which was so brief.

They seem to reminisce forever,
How brave he was, how strong and clever
But I remember, as a kid
How many foolish things he did!

And now, when mother looks at me
It is of him she thinks, I see
And Dad says that when I grow up
Just like him I'll win a cup.

But just to please my Dad and mother
I can't turn myself into my brother
Oh, Mom and Dad why can't you see
I am not him, I'm me, I'm me!

C. Teachers' Questions About the Orphan's Adjustment to a New Reality

The process of mourning of the orphan and of his adjustment to the new reality is very complex and includes various phases. These phases were discussed in chapter two. This process takes place parallel to the orphan's readjustment to his/her class and school after returning from the Shiv'a. Various problems that the teacher will face, but which cannot always be foreseen.

Some of the problems and special situations reported by teachers will be discussed below and an effort will be made to examine ways for the teacher to react in such situations based on consideration of the orphan's special needs. The problems concern the child's process of mourning and severance from the deceased, and his/her readjustment to his/her class. It should be noted that these two different subjects reflect different aspects of the orphan's readjustment to a different reality.

1. Problems Connected to the Process of Mourning and to Severance from the Deceased – *Teachers' Questions*:
   a) A Child in my class, whose father died several months ago,

has changed considerably. He has become withdrawn, distant and introverted. He doesn't play with other children and he doesn't ask me questions. Should I initiate a talk with him about his deceased father?

b) While we were on a nature trip we discovered a dead bird. An orphaned girl burst into tears at the sight. How should I have reacted?

c) When fathers sometimes come to take their children home from school, I can tell that it is hard on Ilan (whose father died). Shall I talk to him about it?

d) A little girl whose father was killed in an accident asked, "What are we going to live on now?" How should I have reacted?

e) Right after the Shiv'a Gilad said to me, "Now I'll have to stop going to physical education classes". What should I have said?

f) Gil (whose father is dead) brought a watch to class one day and, showing it to me, said, "My father bought me this watch". How should I have reacted?

g) A little girl whose mother died is very attached to objects associated with her mother. For instance, she has a pair of gloves which her mother knitted and she won't let anyone touch them. She says, "You can't touch these. My mother made them and now she's dead and no one can make another pair like them".

h) After a visit to the cemetery an orphan asked me, "Why do we go to the cemetry and why do we bring flowers?"

i) A child who is not an orphan asked, "When someone dies, do we have to love him all our lives?"

The first question is the key to the teacher's handling of the orphan in the class. Children vary in their reactions (as expressed in classroom behavior) to the death of someone close to them. Some become withdrawn and introverted (as described in question 1). Others become overly aggressive. Some are given to moods and frequent crying spells and others turn to their teacher to share their pain and fears about the future.

As the questions show, teachers are very sensitive to the changes in the behavior of bereaved children. In most cases, teachers closely observe the bereaved child's behavior in the days following his/her return to school. This observation is accompanied by a certain amount of anxiety as to how they should react if the orphan shows signs of distress and to what extent they should involve themselves in his/her problems.

There were many questions on this subject, of which question 1 is a representative example. We must also consider the question of whether the teacher need worry about how to react if there is no obvious change in the child's behavior after his bereavement. Many teachers feel relieved when a child returns to class after a tragedy and continues as before, showing no sign of change in his/her behavior or attitude. This relief is based on the belief that such behavior is an indication of the child's having recovered from the tragedy, so that the teacher need not actively intervene in a sphere which is so sensitive and so painful. As has been pointed out, however, the period after a parent's death is very difficult for the orphan, whether he/she shows it in his behavior or not. It is a time of pain and grief for the death of someone dear, as well as fear of and anxiety about what the future holds for the orphan and his/her family.

The Picture

When I'm alone and I am sad
I sit and think about my Dad.
And the lonely, empty house
Cries for him because it knows
That he is gone forever.

And suddenly I feel regret ·
That I'm beginning to forget
His face — the face of one so dear.
I'm glad I have his picture near
I'll keep it near forever.

I hold the picture up and gaze
Remembering the bygone days
When he was here.
And as I gaze, and when I see
The face that is so dear to me

I can't believe that suddenly
He's gone from me forever.

During this time processes are taking place which help the bereaved to relinquish the deceased emotionally and to recognize and adjust to the new reality. Even if the child does not initiate a talk with his teacher, and even if his behavior seems normal, the teacher should not interpret this to mean that he/she is capable of going through the mourning process unaided. The child has just encountered a previously unknown phenomenon, and one difficult to understand — death. He/she has experienced pain and grief of an intensity he/she has never experienced before. His/her life has suffered a shock which necessitates reorganization. All this calls for help from adults. The teacher should initiate a talk with the orphan even if he/she doesn't indicate his/her desire to do so. This talk should include the two main aspects of the mourning process; the cognitive (rational) aspect and the emotional aspect.

The teacher should provide a legitimation for the child's pain and understand his/her wishes, even when they are not realistic. The bereaved child should be allowed to talk about the deceased and express his/her feelings. At the same time, the child should be helped to understand the various component elements of the concepts of death. This understanding will serve as the basis for his/her acceptance of his loss and for his/her rebuilding a new reality. The child's expression of his/her anxieties about the future will enable the teacher to help him/her to gain an objective view of the difficulties in store for him/her and to find solutions to problems in which the teacher is able to intervene.

Only A Memory

I am sitting in the back-yard
In the quiet of the evening
Everything is calm and still.

Suddenly I hear my name called
I distinctly hear that dear voice
Though I thought I never will.

Daddy! Daddy! I am trembling
Can it be? My heart is pounding.
I look up and feel a chill.

It is my uncle, Daddy's brother.
I mistook his voice for another
Daddy speaks no more, and never will.

Questions 4 and 5 express the orphan's anxiety about the future. Many orphans are afraid of a change in their economic situation and in their life-style. The shock of losing a parent is great. It is therefore very important that the orphan should feel that with the exception of this fact, all other areas of his life will remain as stable as possible and that his parent's death will not affect them significantly. The family may continue to live in the same home, his/her social life will remain the same, he/she will continue with his various activities as before, and as for the family income, income from various sources may complement the surviving parent's salary.

Questions 2 and 3 describe situations which the orphans associate with the parent's death and absence and which cause them great pain. The teacher should be responsive to instances of a child's expression of pain and grief, and show understanding for those feelings. In addition to responding to the emotional element in the child's reaction, the teacher should seize the opportunity and encourage the child to talk about the deceased, about how he/she feels about him/her, and his/her problems. This is also a good opportunity for the teacher to see how the child conceptualizes death and to clarify its component concepts if necessary.

Questions 6, 7 and 8 reflect the effort of the living to preserve the memory of the dead. Objects and souvenirs of the deceased parent are very important to the child. Sometimes children attribute imagined power and significance to such objects. Such children should be referred for a talk with a psychologist. The teacher should show understanding for the special value that the object has for the child. Beyond its everyday use, the object constitutes a souvenir of the parent and hence its significance. Talking about the child's feeling for the object can lead to talking about the deceased parent and about the child's problems following his/her death. Just like souvenir-objects, visits to the cemetery and putting flowers on the grave satisfy the needs of the living. They cannot benefit or harm the dead. An understanding of the finality of death helps to clarify this point.

Visiting the gravesite is a means of communion with the memory of the deceased and of cherishing this memory. The deceased remains in our memory after our final parting. Throughout the process of accepting the fact of death and of adjusting to a new reality, we (by various means such as objects, pictures and ceremonies) foster this memory.

Chapter 6: Teachers' Questions about the Orphan's Readjustment in the Classroom

1. Should I talk to the class about how they should behave with the orphan when he returns after the Shiv'a?
2. When the class is discussing the family and each child talks about his father's occupation, should I ask an orphan to tell what his deceased father's occupation was?
3. When I'm teaching a story which centers around the character of the father, should I treat it differently than usual if there is an orphan in the class?
4. When the class is making presents for Mother's Day what should I do about a child who lost his mother?
5. On Memorial Day I mentioned the father of one of the children, who was killed in war. I noticed that another orphan in the class, whose father was killed in an accident looked as if he was hurt by the fact that I hadn't mentioned his father, too. How should I have acted?

The second chapter of this book noted the importance of the orphan's class, and particularly his/her teacher, in helping him/her to adjust. The teacher, being an adult who is significant in the child's life, can help by sharing his/her grief, understanding his feelings and initiating talks on the subjects that trouble him/her. The class, being a large peer group, can provide support from the following two directions:

a) The sympathy of non-orphans.
b) The help and support of children who have themselves experienced what the orphan is now going through.

Question 1 reflects the question in many teacher's minds as to how far they should go in actively preparing their class for the return of the orphan. Such preparation is beneficial both for the orphan and for the other children. When a parent of one of the children dies of illness or is killed in an accident, all the children in the class actually experience a degree of mourning. The experience agitates them, is painful and arouses anxieties about themselves and those dear to them. By using this opportunity to clarify the concepts

124

connected with death and by providing legitimation for expression of feeling, the teacher will make it possible for the children to go through a preventive mourning. This will play a vital part in their future ability to deal with the death of someone dear. Preparation develops empathy and sensitivity to the situation of the orphan. The children should become aware of the orphan's pain and of what a difficult time he/she is having. They should learn to be considerate of his/her feelings and should allow him/her to express them. At the same time, they should remember that he/she is still the same child he/she was before, that he/she still likes the same things he/she liked before, and that he/she will continue his/her former friendships and associations.

My Friend — An Orphan

My good friend is now an orphan —
Her father was killed in an accident —

But as soon as the mourning was done
She returned to be just like every one
She's the same in school, she's the same at play
She whispers, she giggles, she's cheerful and gay.

She gossips and fights with us
She shares our delights with us
She's butterfly wings
She dances and sings.

Only sometimes she goes off by herself
And my heart aches for her, all by herself,
But I know at that moment she'd rather
Be alone with the memory of her father.

Unfortunately, almost no thought has so far been devoted in the school curriculum to the subject of death. Despite this, the curriculum as it is, provides the teacher with many opportunities of working on the subject, of talking about what it means to be an orphan, and of developing sensitivity to and understanding of the needs of the orphaned child. Such opportunities are varied, and may be directly connected to the subject. Memorial Day is an example. Other occasions may be only idirectly related to it — for instance Mother's Day, the subject of the family, or stories and poems whose main characters are central family figures. The guiding principle in answering all the teacher's questions on this subject is that the presence of orphans in the class must not be ignored and their problems must be recognized.

Changing emphasis in a story built around the character of the father in order not to 'hurt' the orphan is doubly harmful, because it teaches the orphan that his/her position is so shameful that it must be hidden. The child will feel that not only is the fact of his/her father's death being ignored but that every possible way is being taken in order not to face the problem. The orphan's need to share his/her problems with his teacher has already been noted. A story whose central character is the father presents a good opportunity for discussing the situation of a child who has no father. Such a discussion makes the orphan feel that his teacher and the other children accept him/her as he/she is and that his/her being an orphan is not a stigma. It gives him/her an opportunity to express his feelings and doubts, and it serves to develop the empathy of the other children.

A situation in which children tell about their father's occupation while studying the subject of the family, enables the orphan to tell the other children about his father when he was alive and to convey the message that he/she had a father, just like them, what his father's occupation was, and he is therefore not so different from them. On Mother's day, the orphaned child cannot, of course, make a present for his/her dead mother, nor should he write her a letter. He can, however, make a present for someone else to whom he/she chooses to give it. The teacher can use the opportunity for a talk with the class about an orphan's problems; how he gets along without his/her mother, what his/her problems are, etc. The children might explore possible solutions to problems that an orphan encounters because he/she has no mother.

Summation

Death is a natural phenomenon which is inevitable and central in the life of every human being. Children, too, are preoccupied with

126

death, whether because they have experienced a direct encounter with death by losing someone dear or because they have encountered it indirectly and are troubled by questions to which they have no answer. Children need help from adults in working through their mourning and emotional support while going through the mourning process. Such help and support are essential in the orphan's readjustment. Talks and explanations to non-orphans on the subject of death are vital for their understanding of the subject, for avoiding unrealistic fantasies about death, and for building up the child's 'immunity'. This will enable him to deal with death if and when he/she encounters it personally.

The first chapter of this book stressed the importance of the teacher in the child's life. Because death is a subject difficult for parents to deal with, it is important for the teacher to acknowledge and talk about children's fears and anxieties in connection with death and to help them gain a realistic perspective of the subject. This depends on the child's age and intelligence level.

The second chapter discussed the problems of the orphan at school and stressed the class as a source of help and support for the orphan. The widow (or widower) is not always able to help the orphan in his mourning, because of her/his own grief and because unlike the teacher, she/he doesn't always know what the child's needs are at this time. The teacher, on the other hand, possesses the tools (the knowledge and the opportunity) to help the orphan, both in the process of working through the mourning and in his/her readjustment at school. In addition, the teacher has recourse to the advice of other experts who can help him/her. The fact that the teacher's approach sometimes contradicts the parent's should not prevent the teacher from acting. The parent naturally wants to protect the child from pain and therefore sometimes tells the child what he/she wishes were the truth ("Daddy is in heaven looking down at you all the time"). The teacher can explain to the child that such statements are not lies, but rather wishes of the parent. It is natural to feel that way but it must not be considered as the truth. The dead continue to exist only in the memory of the living. Since they are dead, they cannot look down at us as living people do.

It must be remembered that in addition to teachers there are other individuals and institutions, whose function it is to render support to bereaved families and who are able to help the orphan work through his mourning. It is important that the teacher be in contact with such institutions. He may turn to them for professional counseling on problems with which he cannot deal alone. Such contact makes possible the exchange of information on the child's adjustment in the various spheres of his life (home, school) and joint planning of ways to help the orphan achieve optimal adjustment.

Being widowed in early adulthood and orphaned in early childhood is an anomalous situation which creates many problems. The teacher might often find it impossible to deal with these problems alone, although it is his/her task to help the orphan, and to a certain extent to help the family, the teacher must remember that there are other professionals who share the task of helping the family. If they are not to be found in the immediate environment, he should try to locate them, work with them, or refer the family to them. Sometimes the teacher himself may need professional help while working with an orphan or on the subject of death.

Part Four:

SCHOOL INVOLVEMENT AND ACTION ON THE SUBJECT OF DEATH

Chapter 1: Significance of School Involvement

The previous chapter dealt with the orphan's mourning process and with the teacher's possible involvement in this process in order to help the child. The present chapter will try to elaborate and to present a model of school involvement, encompassing the entire school and all its component elements, with the teacher playing his part.

Children spend many hours at school and come in contact with various teachers and staff members, such as the principal and the school nurse etc. They are sometimes helped by members of the specialized staff such as the resource teacher, classroom teacher, tutor, counselor, school psychologist and school social worker. The concept of 'school' therefore, involves a broad range of implications as far as activities, relationships and persons affecting the child are concerned. It is reasonable to suppose that all the child's significant experiences – including the death of a parent – will have some connection with one or more of the various component elements of the school system. According to the suggested model for school involvement, therefore, it is not the teacher alone, but rather the entire school system, that reacts to the orphaned child and his family.

As the first step, we shall try to justify the model from the following three viewpoints.

1. The significance of school involvement for the orphan.
2. The significance of school involvement for the bereaved family.
3. The significance of school involvement for the teacher.

A. The Significance of School Involvement for the Orphan

Like the other school children, the orphan comes into contact with various elements of the school. He is under the supervision of his homeroom teacher and several other teachers. He sometimes visits the school nurse, he comes in contact with the principal, he has talks with the school counselor, and he may sometimes need help from the special staff — resource teacher, social worker, or psychologist. It is natural that the nature of the child's relationship with each of these different people is different. With some he is close, he feels he can share his problems with them and turn to them for help, while with others he is withdrawn, indifferent, or even afraid. In addition to the relationship with various adults, the orphan comes into daily close contact with his peers. He studies with them, competes with them for a position in the class, plays with them, talks to them.

The tragedy of a parent's death has inevitable and far reaching implications for the child. His reality has suddenly changed and he must struggle with intense emotional difficulties. His functioning at school will necessarily be affected by this in some way. All those who come into contact with him, adults and children alike, will become aware of and be affected by the change that has taken place in him. Moreover, the very knowledge of the fact of a death in a classmate's family will cause agitation among the other children, and will give rise to questions about the right way to behave with the orphan and with his family. Children and teachers will wonder whether to talk to the orphan about his loss. His teacher will wonder whether to visit the family or to invite the surviving parent for a talk, etc.

Since many component elements in the school system share the same doubts about their reaction to the orphaned child and to his tragedy, it would be desirable that all these elements assume an integrated involvement. The school must react and convey to the child and to his family a sense of consideration for and sensitivity to their pain. At the same time the school must convey its confidence in their ability to recover from the tragedy and readjust. It is un-thinkable that the death be ignored because people find it difficult and embarrassing to speak about it. It is important that the orphan should know that everyone at school knows about the death in his family (his teachers, the principal, the nurse, all the children, etc.) and that it is not a secret that he must hide. It is important that he should feel that others sympathize with him and are ready to support and help him, but have no wish to turn him into an object of pity.

The orphan will turn to those members of the staff to whom he feels closest for a talk, to ask questions and express his feelings. This may not always be his current homeroom teacher, and it is therefore important for other staff members, – the counselor, for instance – to maintain contact with the child and provide the possibility for him to turn to them. The advantage of members of the school staff over members of the family in helping the orphan at this stage of his mourning lies in the fact that they are not directly involved in the tragedy. In addition they have had professional training. It is difficult to expect of a brother or an uncle to be able to explain matters connected with death and to help the child work through his feelings resulting from the loss, at a time when he is dealing with his own distress.

In conclusion, an integrated reaction on the part of the school will significantly affect the orphan's mourning process and his readjustment. This was confirmed by interviews with adults who had been orphaned in childhood.*

An 18-year-old subject who lost her father as a result of an illness when she was 11 said, "One of my teachers came to me on her own initiative and talked to me, on a personal level, about the significance of death. This teacher had herself lost her daughter and this fact made me feel close to her... During this talk I burst into tears and for the first time I was able to find some relief from my pain."

A similar sense of gratitude to a teacher who visited her during the Shiv'a was expressed by another subject, who was orphaned at the age of 10. "I still remember the visit of my piano teacher during our Shiv'a. That may have been the reason for my close relationship with her afterwards and for the fact that I continued playing the piano despite my initial intention to stop because of the tragedy."

* In a study which we conducted in 1980, in which 72 adults were interviewed. See also page 141 "Interviews with Adults Orphaned in Childhood."

Some of the subjects expressed ambivalent feelings to the visits of a teacher or a principal to the bereaved family: "Classmates came to visit me and so did my teacher," said a 24-year-old subject who lost her father when she was 10. "On one hand I was terribly embarrassed because I felt the teacher came out of pity for me and because she thought it was her duty, but on the other hand it was important to me that she took the trouble."

"Looking back, I see that it was important that my teacher came and if she hand't come I would have been hurt. But then, at the time, I felt that her visit was of no significance because I didn't feel particularly close to that teacher and I felt it was just a courtesy visit. Also, the teacher didn't talk about the tragedy or about my future. She sat silently and her silence oppressed me." These are the words of a subject who had lost her mother when she was 12.

Another subject said, "My homeroom teacher called me and we talked about the accident in which my father was killed. At first I felt angry with him for invading my privacy, but afterwards I gave a lot of thought to this talk, and I felt that it brought me closer to him. After that I talked to him about many other things."

The ambivalence towards the teacher's visit as expressed in the examples above appears to stem from two causes. One is the embarrassment and discomfort aroused by the subject of death in general and the social taboo that still prevails in connection with the subject. This creates a certain amount of tension both in the orphan and in the adults around him, as they grope for the right thing to say to him. However, this embarrassment must not deter adults from dealing with the matter. The subjects of the study testified to how significant the visits of members of the school staff were for them, and how helpful the talks which they initiated were, despite the emotional strain involved. We must, however, find ways to reduce the tension and discomfort of adults and children alike.

Another cause for the ambivalence, which was implied in the examples above, is the fact that the homeroom teacher might not always be the right person to visit the orphan and have a talk with him. What is important is the degree of closeness of the adult to the child, his personal touch, and his capacity for frankness. Sometimes the child might feel closer to another member of the staff — a former teacher, the school nurse, the principal, etc.

Some subjects told of their disappointment in the behavior of members of the school staff. A 17-year-old subject who lost his mother when he was 12 said, "We knew that death was near because mother was very ill. Before she died the school counselor called me in for a number of talks which were very helpful. But after mother's death the talks stopped and she never called me in again..."

"The school principal telephoned me", said another subject, who lost his father when he was 15, "...he said that he was shocked to hear of our tragedy and apologized for not being able to come in person because we lived so far away... I was very hurt by this, because he could have come by bus. I was also hurt by the fact that no teachers and almost no friends from school came to visit me. I suppose they were afraid to come..."

The last two examples illustrate how much the orphan needs and looks forward to a response on the part of the school to his tragedy.

A subject who lost her mother when she was 12 added an important point: "I remember how hard it was for me to go back to school at the beginning of the school year. My mother died during the summer vacation and none of the children in my class came to visit me. My teacher didn't come to visit me. I didn't know if they knew and I didn't know how they would react. I think it is very important for the teacher to visit the home of the orphan, both as a personal response and as a means of maintaining contact between the orphan and the framework of his class and school..."

Thus, in addition to the simple, human significance of a teacher's visit to the home of a bereaved child, such a visit has another, long-range implication. It helps the orphan to return to normal life and to make a better adjustment. As one subject expressed it, "It is important that they come – principals, teachers and classmates – because it gives the orphan a feeling of life going on, it shows him that his life has not been rent..."

A number of the subjects referred to how essential it was for the school staff to participate in the child's mourning: "I recommend that teachers as well as classmates come to call during the Shiv'a"; "It is advisable that the teacher should talk to the class about the death, because after such a talk they will understand the orphan better, they will behave more naturally with him, and they will not show him pity"; "It is important that friends come to call during the Shiv'a. It gives you the feeling that others care and it takes your mind off your pain".

To conclude, based on the personal experience of people who were orphaned in childhood, there is no doubt that the participation of members of the school staff in a child's mourning is of great importance. It is a human act of caring, of sharing the child's pain, and it should be viewed as part of the professional responsibility of every member of the staff.

B. The Significance of School Involvement for the Bereaved Family

The members of the bereaved family, and particularly the widow (or widower) are aware of the part that the school plays in the child's life. During the years of her child's attendance in a school, a mother generally becomes acquainted with the staff and her child's classmates through parent-teacher meetings, school trips and celebrations. Despite the changes which have taken place in the education system and in the way it is viewed, a lot of responsibility over the child is still attributed to the school. Parents generally view the school as an institution which educates the child and shapes his character, rather than only a means of importing knowledge. For this reason a response of the school to the family's bereavement is to be desired. It conveys the message that the school is a source of support, and help, and guidance. The various staff members can put themselves at the disposal of the bereaved family and respond to the needs which arise from the tragedy. The widow (or widower) has probably previously established some relationship with one of the staff members and he would naturally be the one to help her/him and her/his child. It must be remembered that the surviving parent and other members of the family are themselves going through a crisis and may not be able to behave with the child in a reasoned and well advised manner. In such an instance other adults, who are not directly involved in the tragedy and who are professionally trained and experienced, can help the entire family, including the child, to deal with the situation.

C. The Significance of School Involvement for the Teacher

All that has been said about the teacher's role and possible contribution in helping the orphan and his family is valid and important. However, the teacher must be viewed as one element in an entire system. He is not the only one who carries the responsibility of responding to the child's tragedy:

a) As has been pointed out, the child has associations with others of the school staff besides the teacher. They all affect the child, though the nature and intensity of their relationship with him varies. All that happens to the child affects the staff members who come into contact with him, and therefore an event such as the death of a parent concerns them as much as it does the teacher.

b) The homeroom teacher is usually the closest to the child and thus particularly significant. However, precisely this emotional closeness and involvement may sometimes hinder him in the role of helping the child in a crisis.

c) There is no justification for imposing all responsibility on one particular member of the school staff. The teacher carries responsibility for the entire class and must deal with the effect of one child's tragedy on the other children in the class. Moreover, the teacher is not usually trained and experienced in dealing with crises such as a death in the family. On the other hand, there are people on the school staff who are better trained to deal with such situations — the counselor, the social worker, the psychologist, etc. It is important that these contribute their skills in helping both the teacher and the child and his family to deal with the situation, whether they do this directly or indirectly.

In conclusion, it may be assumed that in a situation where the teacher doesn't feel that he stands alone in his effort to help the orphaned child and his family, he will feel more relaxed and be able to work more willingly and efficiently.

Chapter 2: Ways in Which the School Can Help the Orphan

The previous chapter described the ways in which the teacher can help the orphaned child throughout the various stages of his mourning; from the moment of notification through the funeral, the Shiv'a, the visit to the gravesite and the talk about the deceased. This section will examine the ways in which the entire school, with its various component elements, can help the orphan and his family in the stages mentioned above.

1. If the school is notified of the death during morning hours, the principal should notify all staff members who come in contact with the child. At the same time he can learn which member of the staff knows the child and his family best and has the closest relationship with the child. In addition to the person chosen to deal with the situation another staff member (or members) can be asked to help him to notify the child, to accompany him home and to deal with the family.

It is important that during this encounter with the family, and particularly the surviving parent, the staff member should inform them that the child has been told of the death. The following information should be conveyed:

a) That the child should be told the truth about everything connected with the death. The facts should be presented to him simply and clearly, in accordance with his level of understanding.

b) That the school is aware of the tragedy and sympathizes with the family.

c) That the members of the school staff are ready to render any advice and assistance necessary, and that they have the knowledge and the experience necessary to deal with such situations.

2. The orphan's class should be notified of their friend's tragedy. The person who informs the class should be the staff member closest to that class, with the possible participation of a member of the special staff. Together they can answer any questions that the children might ask in connection with the tragedy and its significance and deal with any emotional reactions which the children might display. It is important that such questions or reactions from the children

136

meet with a suitable response on preventive action. The children must see that death can be talked about like any other subject, and that it is legitimate to ask questions and show feelings about it. Conveying this message to the children is particularly important, because in many families talking freely and naturally about death is not allowed.

3. It is important that the principal, the homeroom teacher and other staff members who know the child attend the funeral. It is also desirable that, after the class has been suitably prepared, some of the orphan's classmates attend the ceremony.

4. It should be clearly conveyed to the orphan and to the surviving parent that staying home during the Shiv'a and discontinuing his normal routine is important for the child. The possible undesirable effects on the child of coming to school during Shiv'a should be explained. The family should also be told to expect a visit from some of the school staff and some of the orphan's classmates during the Shiv'a. The significance of such a visit to the child should be explained.

5. When the child returns to school he will have various problems and difficulties. In order to limit the number of these problems and their severity, the child should be called in for a talk. It should be made clear to him that the school is aware of and understands the crisis he is going through and that no one expects him to return immediately to his former level of functioning. However, he should try gradually to return to normal in his studies and social activities, with various staff members available to help him. The child should be asked to decide which staff member he would prefer and a regular schedule of meetings with that person should be set.

6. In the second stage of school involvement, a follow-up should be conducted on the child's situation and level of functioning at school. In addition, contact should be maintained with the child's family and there should be an exchange of information on how the child is dealing with the crisis.

The child should be made aware of what will be expected and required of him as time goes on. If necessary he and his family should be referred to experts for help. The contact with the surviving parent should be maintained − not for therapeutic purposes (there are experts to whom he can be referred for that), but to show interest and caring even after the crisis is over. This will make the family feel that the school cares, and will engender a positive atmosphere in the family and a positive attitude to the school as a source of support.

7. On the initiative of the counselor, the resource teacher or the school psychologist special ideas and projects can be implemented for the purpose of preventive action on the subject of death. For instance, regular group meetings might be held for orphans in the school. Such meetings would serve to reduce the sense of loneliness, to develop new friednships based on a common experience, and to encourage expression of feelings and thoughts in an atmosphere of understanding. In addition, the orphans can learn from each other different ways of dealing effectively with similar problems.

Another possibility is for one of the staff members to organize a preventive program on various subjects, including death. He can do this by himself or with the cooperation and help of the homeroom teachers. The program might include presenting the subject through a film or a story, using special teaching methods, or in response to some current event. After the presentation a discussion should take place, during which questions can be asked and conceptions clarified, and feelings aroused by the subject can be expressed.

Members of the educational staff or parents often ask whether dealing with the subject of death in class may not have adverse effects on the non-orphan children and whether such activities as outlined above may not be harmful for them. The answer to such questions is unequivocally negative.

Chapter 3: Dealing With the Subject of Death in School is Beneficial for Non-Orphans

An understanding of mental health and practical experience in the matter, inevitably lead one to the conclusion that dealing with the subject of death in school, provided it is done properly, is beneficial and helpful to the orphan as well as to non-orphans. This conclusion is based on the following three reasons:

1. In case of a parent's death, the other children will be preoccupied with the subject in any case. They will hear it talked about, and they will think about it, and perhaps even dream about it. They may discuss it among themselves, and it may arouse disturbing feelings. The subject will arise in any case, and a response on the part of the school is called for and justifiable. Rather than risk misconceptions and false and frightening conclusions on the part of the children, it is better to deal with the subject and assure the proper attitude to it.

2. Death is difficult to grasp and it arouses anxiety. The death of a person who is not close to the child provides an opportunity to deal with the subject on the cognitive as well as on the emotional level. It serves as preparation and "immunization" in case of a future closer encounter with death. It is safe to assume that a child who has had the opportunity to ask questions and to express his feelings about death, will deal more effectively with a case of death in the future.

3. By means of active initiatives on the part of the school in dealing with death and open discussion of the subject, the message is conveyed to the children that death is a legitimate topic of discussion. As with other sensitive and embarrassing subjects in our culture and society, it is important that we learn to free ourselves of reservations and inhibitions and develop an openness and a willingness to express our feelings and thoughts more freely.

In conclusion: School intervention following a parent's death is beneficial and helpful to the orphan as well as to the non-orphans.

Summation

The model of school intervention described above is based on our accumulated experience in working with orphans and with their families. It is largely based on the idea of preventive action in the community, the essence of which is preventive initiatives in the sphere of physical and mental health. Its purpose is to prevent the inception of problems or to prevent their aggravation.

The school is conceived of as a powerful and influential educational-supportive system. It comprises a staff of various professionals, possessing a range of expertise, experience and personal qualities. Such a system is capable of making a contribution in helping bereaved families to deal with their crisis, through direct action with the orphan and his family, by discovering problems and referring those in need of help to outside experts, and through direct intervention with the children of the class.

It must be remembered that any model is based on generalizations and should be viewed merely as a basic principle and as a guideline. Each school must be flexible in the kind of action it decides to take. Each school is different in the composition of its staff and their skills, their qualifications, and their personalities. Each school is different in the general atmosphere which prevails in it, in the amount of initiative and openness it shows in implementing new educational initiatives, in its status in the community, and in its needs. In addition to all these, before any action is taken, the character of the individual bereaved family must be taken into consideration.

We are of the opinion that the educational staff of a school should develop a plan of action, both preventive and interventive, to be implemented in case of death in a child's family. If the action is based on the principles of the framework and model described and on the specific needs dictated by every school situation, they will find it much easier to act when the need arises. Advance thought and planning, free of the pressures of a crisis, and special training given to some of the school staff will prove very worthwhile.

Part 5:

INTERVIEWS WITH ADULTS ORPHANED IN CHILDHOOD

A. Aim of the interviews

The aim of this chapter is to enable the reader to learn directly from the experience of people who were orphaned in their child-hood and from their suggestions of how the family and school can help the orphan.

Seventy two adults took part in this study. Each of them had lost either father or mother in childhood. The nine interviews pre-sented below constitute a random sample of this study, representing the interviews with one out of every eight subjects. Each subject received a letter asking him to participate in the study. It was worded as follows:

"We are conducting a study on the adjustment difficulties of orphaned children. One of the aims of our study is to find ways of preventing difficulties and of helping orphans in their development and adjustment. One of the sources from which we would like to learn are the orphans themselves, or rather adults who were orphaned in childhood. Would you be willing to attend two interview sessions and help us learn from your personal experience how to help orphans?"

B. Questions asked in the interviews of 72 adults, orphaned in childhood

The interview consisted of 12 questions. In the first session each subject answered the first three questions and in the second session, the remaining nine. The answers were recorded by the interviewer.

Following are the twelve questions asked in the interview:

1. As far as you can remember, what aspect of being orphaned was the most difficult for you to deal with?

2. As far as you can remember, what were the things that helped you?

3. What are your suggestions for alleviating the orphan's suffering and enhancing his ability to adjust?

4. Should his parent's death be concealed from a child for a while or should he be notified immediately? How should the child be notified?

5. Should children be taken to the funeral?

6. Should children be taken to visit the gravesite?

7. Should children of non-religious families be sent to school during the Shiv'a or should they be kept at home?

8. When you think of yourself after having been orphaned, do you remember yourself as being different from other children? If so, in what way were you different?

9. Do you think it is advisable for the widow/widower to invite friends of the opposite sex into the house?

10. Did the fact that your surviving parent was a widow/widower represent a hardship to you? If so, how?

11. In your opinion, is it to the orphan's advantage that the surviving parent remarry?

12. Do you recall any fears you had after being orphaned?

The reader can read the answers to the questions in one of two ways: He can read all 12 answers of each subject, to gain an understanding of that particular subject; or he can read the answers of all the subjects to one particular question, if that particular question is what interests him.

Interview of Subject No. 1

A 21-year-old university student who lost her father when she was 10.

Question 1

My father died of cancer after having been hospitalized for about half a year. When he was hospitalized, my mother took over the management of his business and was away from home for most of the day. In addition, we used to go to the hospital every day to visit my father. Despite the fact that I knew about my father's illness and often heard people say that he was going to die, the significance of what it means to die was not clear to me. No one explained to me that after he died, my father would never return. No one talked to me about the funeral either.

My main difficulty was that I was expected to be grown up beyond my age. I was entrusted with the housekeeping, and I felt that I had lost not only my father, but, since she was away working all day, also my mother. I began to quarrel with my mother and these quarrels intensified during my adolescence. Mother always expected me to have everything in the house done when she returned from work – the shopping, the cooking, the cleaning. We never had a chance to talk. Mother used to cry when father was mentioned, so in the first years after his death he was hardly ever mentioned. And mother was always working hard and always tired. I wanted very much for her to remarry, so I could again have a father, and a mother. It used to bother me when I visited friends and saw normal family relations and expressions of warmth and tenderness. I would return from such visits even more bitter than before. I wanted so much to have a family like other children.

Question 2

One thing that helped me was that I never hid the fact that I was an orphan, but I did remove his picture from my room, after some friends who visited me were embarrassed when they asked where he was and I answered that he was dead. Another thing that helped me was the fact that my big brother who was 18, to a certain extent played the role of father to me. We had no financial difficulties, and I suppose that helped too.

Question 3

I think the most important thing is to maintain the family framework after the death, because there is no substitute for the sense of warmth and protection that provides for the orphan. In addition, I think it is important for the surviving parent to get professional counseling so that, despite his own difficulties, he will know how to behave with his children, how to explain things and how to help them. The orphan should remain with his family, but the surviving parent should make it clear to him that he is suffering too, to allow the child to share his pain, and with the help of professional counseling to go through the period of mourning together.

Question 4

Death is such an intangible, even for adults. You can't touch death. It is even difficult to feel death. Therefore, in my opinion, the notification of death should take the form of an explanation and be done in stages. However, it must begin immediately after the death, and the child must not be decieved with stories about places his deceased parent has gone to. Notifying the child of the truth clearly now saves problems later.

When it happened in our family, my brother called and asked to talk to my mother. I joked with him on the phone but he was nervous and asked for mother. Mother took the phone and immediately began crying. She didn't say a thing. I was afraid to cry but I immediately understood that father had died. I ran upstairs to our neighbor, calling to mother, "I'm going to tell our neighbor" and there I burst out crying.

Question 5

I don't know if children should be taken to the funeral or not. The funeral makes the death more real but it is an extremely painful experience. The child shouldn't be forced to go, but it seems strange to suggest it. The child should not be told that he isn't being allowed to attend the funeral because it is a difficult experience. Actually, I don't know how the situation should be handled, but I do know that the child's presence at the funeral and his seeing the burial are important, even if the child is very young.

My mother felt strongly that I should attend the funeral. I was taken and that was that. No one asked me, and I think that was good for me. At the cemetery I showed a lot of curiosity and interest. Everyone was crying and pitying me, I was just a poor little girl. They kissed me and pointed at me – it was ridiculous.

Question 6

The gravesite and the tombstone are much more sterile and less disturbing than the funeral but they are important in actualizing death too. No matter what age, children should be taken to the gravesite as soon after death as possible, but after a suitable preparation. The surviving parent and the orphan must work through what happened together. It is important for them to cry together at the gravesite, and that makes crying legitimate for each one of them.

I went to the cemetery with mother during the Shiv'a and on the month anniversary of father's death, to honor his memory. It was important to me that the gravesite be clean and well kept. That is important to the family – the living. I felt that despite the fact that my father was dead, he had his place in our family, so I always took part in washing down the tombstone, cleaning around the gravesite, putting flowers on the grave, etc. We used to do this before memorial ceremonies at the gravesite, so that it would be more pleasant to come there.

Question 7

It's hard for me to give an unequivocal answer. It seems to me that the child should be asked if he wants to stay home all week. All in all, it's a very difficult week, a week of uninterrupted, intensive mourning. If the child stays home, he should be allowed to spend a few hours each day away from home. Basically, it is important not to cut the child off from what is happening. He should be part of things and share them, but he should be the one to decide where he will be − in his own room or with all the adults.

I stayed home throughout the Shiv'a and the friends who came to visit me sat with me in my room. My teacher came too, which embarrassed me greatly because I felt that she had come out of a sense of duty and because she pitied me, but on the other hand, it was important to me that she responded to my tragedy.

Question 8

I was certainly different from other children. My responsibilities were tenfold. My mother charged me with responsibilities that other children my age didn't even dream of and what's more, she was never satisfied with how I carried them out. I had to play the role of secretary, housekeeper, messenger, and perform many other tasks. It was a great burden, and my efforts were never appreciated.

The other children neither made things difficult nor easy for me. I remember only one time when a boy from the neighborhood said, after we had had a fight, "I wish your mother were dead, too". I almost tore out his ear for that. I still remember his screams.

146

Question 9

I think my mother used her healthy intuition in this matter. She always said that we must adjust and rebuild our lives. Life must go on. She explained to me that her remarrying would be good for me too. She said she would gain a new husband and I would gain a whole family. She said her second husband would not be my father nor take my father's place but would be someone who was good to me and love me.

My mother never met her dates outside of the house. She always insisted that they come to our home and meet me, and understand that I was part of the bargain. If a man was not able to accept me, he had no chance of marrying my mother. I wanted mother to remarry so that we would become a family again. It seemed like a good solution for all of us.

I think it is important that a widow should invite men into her home. It is essential. I think a widow should present remarriage to her children as a desirable thing, as my mother did.

Question 10

In retrospect, I think that my mother's being widowed developed my independence and advanced my development. I learned to keep house, to take care of banking business, of insurance, etc. I used to got to deposit money at the bank at the age of 11. My mother would give me large sums of money to deposit. I once asked her if she wasn't afraid I'd lose the money and she answered that she relied on me.

Nevertheless, I would advise widows not to impose such a heavy burden on young children, not to demand so much of them, because it makes them feel even more different from other children. I would also advise them to establish a dialogue with their children and an atmosphere of sharing the grief and the pain caused by death.

Question 11

My mother remarried when I was 14. There is no harm to the orphan in the remarriage of his surviving parent. My mother explained the importance of her remarriage well in advance of the event itself, so that everything was gradual. She went out with my stepfather for some time, she allowed me to share her feelings, asked me if I liked him and what about him I didn't like, so that I felt part of this new relationship and I liked the idea.

Question 12

I was afraid then and I still am of mother's dying too. When mother is late or doesn't let me know where she went, I'm hysterical with fear that something has happened to her.

The subject is a 26-year-old woman, a university graduate, and married. She lost her father when she was 13.

Question 1

Several things were difficult for me: First and foremost was the fact that I didn't have a father while other children did. I was so jealous of children who had a father, that I found it difficult to visit the home of my best girl friend and see a whole, happy family as mine used to be before my father died. I used to sit by myself and daydream about the happy family I had once had, and more than once I would run out of the house crying, begging my father to return so that I could hear my mother laugh again and we could all be happy once more.

Another problem was the fact that I was pitied and that people were afraid to talk to me not only about my father but about their fathers, so as not to remind me. The result was that when I went to high school I didn't tell anyone that my father was dead, and when people asked me where my father worked I would say he worked for the Ministry of Defense.

Question 2

What helped me was that the family remained as it had been — we had always been a united family, we always helped one another and had a lot of fun together. We remained that way and helped one another to overcome the terrible loss.

Question 3

I'm not sure what to answer. Today I think that it would have been better if I had talked more about father. My problem was that when I talked about him it was to myself. When we used to talk about father at home, and we did it often, my mother always used to cry. As a result, sometimes when I felt like talking about him I preferred not to, so that mother wouldn't cry. I didn't talk to my brother either and outside the house I preferred that people didn't know. I preferred to avoid embarrassing situations such as, "What does your father do?" – "My father is dead" – "Oh, I'm so sorry", etc.

When my homeroom teacher called me for a talk on the subject, I was angry because I felt he was invading my privacy. Nevertheless, I later gave a lot of thought to our talk, I felt closer to my teacher, and it helped me that every so often he would find the time to ask me how I was getting along.

Question 4

The child should be notified immediately. He has a right to know what happened and how it happened. This is how it was with me.

I was visiting a girl-friend. It was about 9 o'clock in the evening and I was waiting for my parents to pick me up. Suddenly the doorbell rang. I opened the door and saw my mother looking frightened. She asked, "Is your father here?" and when I answered no she said, "Then you no longer have a father". I didn't understand what she was talking about. Then she burst into tears and told my girl-friend's parents that there had been an accident in the street outside, that an ambulance had already picked up the victim and that the driver had said he was dead. She said this amidst terrible sobs.

Then my mother and my girl-friend's mother went to the hospital to identify the body. I was left in my girl-friend's house, and I still didn't understand what had happened. Later I was taken home, where many of the family were already assembled. My mother was already home. I was angry that she hadn't taken me with her to the hospital so that I too could say goodbye to father. Mother asked me to sit by her side but I refused and I didn't go near her all evening.

Question 5

In my opinion children should attend the funeral to help them understand what happened. It is undoubtedly a very difficult experience, but the child should experience it. It is very hard for the child to grasp what has happened, particularly if the death was sudden — yesterday your father was alive and today he's being buried. The funeral makes it more real. It forces you to face reality.

For me the funeral ceremony symbolized a farewell — my parting from my father. I didn't cry, I stood frozen and looked on. In my heart, I was talking to father. Children should be taken to the funeral. They shouldn't be asked if they want to go. They should be made to feel that it is the natural thing to do. Father has died and everyone is to attend his funeral. If the child refuses to go, he should not be forced to, but an effort should be made to persuade him, by understanding explanations.

I remember that I was awoken and found the house full of people. I was told that we were going to the funeral and we went. I don't remember whether I was prepared beforehand or whether I had any reservations about going. I only remember my aunt waking me and the house full of people.

Question 6

I visit my father's gravesite often, and I shall continue to do so. I go every year for the gravesite memorial service, whenever my mother wants to, and whenever an important event in my life is about to happen or has happened. When something happens that is important to me I 'share' it with my father. The day before I was married I took my husband to visit the cemetery. I felt I was notifying my father of my marriage and introducing my future husband to him. I felt that this visit also gave my husband a more complete picture of who I am, including my relationship with my father.

In my opinion children should be taken to visit the gravesite, and soon after the tragedy, so that they can better grasp what has happened.

Question 7

As I have said already, the child should be allowed to share in everything and it should be done naturally, as a matter of course. He should not be asked and confronted with decisions. He should stay home during the Shiv'a, with the rest of the family. If the child asks not to stay, that is a different matter. I wasn't asked, I stayed home with my mother and brother, and I think that is how it should be.

I remember that children and teachers from my school attended the funeral and that it was important to me that they did. None of the teachers came during the Shiv'a and only two of my girlfriends came, but many of my brother's friends filled the house at all times and that helped him a lot, and me too. I preferred to sit with them, and be able to smile sometimes, rather than be with the adults, who were crying most of the time.

Question 8

I felt different in that I did not have a father and the other children did. I was jealous of them and I tried hard to hide the fact that I was an orphan in order not to be different.

Question 9

There has never been another man in our house. Mother is still 'married' to father. However, I think I would have been glad if there had been, and both my brother and I have been encouraging my mother for years to marry again.

Question 10

It bothered me a lot. I was haunted by the thought that my mother was to be pitied (much more than myself), I felt sorry for her and worried about her. That is why I never left her at home alone,

I never slept over at a girlfriend's house and I never went on trips with friends. My mother never asked me to do that, she was strong and encouraged me, but I felt I wanted to and that I owed it to her. I felt I owed it to her because I still had my life in front of me while hers was behind her. Maybe that's why I always wanted her to remarry, so that I could be relieved of the responsibility.

Question 11

The question is hypothetical for me because I haven't experienced what my mother's remarriage would be like for me, but I have a clearcut opinion on the matter. If there is someone else, the fact must not be hidden from the child. A child should be part of what happens in his family and know everything that's going on. The widow must decide for herself about remarriage. She must think about her future. Of course it is to be desired that the relations between the children and their stepfather be good, but the decision should be the mother's alone. Children can be egotistical, and may not be willing to accept a substitute for their father. In such a case, the mother must think of herself and of the day when her children will leave home and she will remain alone.

Question 12

I was afraid that something would happen to my mother or to my brother. I was afraid that I would be left without them and have to go through the terrible time that followed my father's death again.

Interview of Subject No. 3

The subject is 24 years-old, a high school graduate, lost his mother when he was 6. She died after a long illness.

Question 1

I don't remember anything that was particularly difficult in the period after my mother's death. I was very young and probably didn't grasp the situation fully. Also, it didn't come suddenly. My mother was seriously ill for a very long time and during this time a gradual detachment took place between us. Several months before she died I was placed in a kibbutz, with some relatives. I was with a family that I knew and I had always liked staying with them. My being an orphan bothered me more when I was older. On the kibbutz I didn't feel different from the other children. On a kibbutz all the children are more detached from their parents*, and when the others used to go to visit with their families I would go and visit with my foster family. As I have said, this was a family I knew since I could remember myself and they loved me. But, afterwards, when I returned to the city and entered high school, it bothered me to be branded an orphan. I had the feeling that the label 'orphan' was the foremost element in my identity. That is why I didn't want to tell anyone that I was an orphan. I preferred to evade questions on the subject, so that I wouldn't seem different. I myself did not consider myself different, and I didn't think that I behaved differently from others because of the fact that I was orphaned in early childhood. Since I was afraid that others would attribute some things in my behavior to my being an orphan, I preferred to conceal the fact.

---

* Because they live away from their parents and with children of their age group.

Question 2

First of all, I didn't feel forsaken. I knew I had my family – my father and brothers – behind me. I knew they would do everything to take care of me. I admired and adored them. It was important for me to see that my family overcame its tragedy and was functioning well. I even had the feeling that my family was special (and there were people who told me so) in its success in rehabilitating itself after all that it had suffered. Another thing that helped me was the fact that I was on the kibbutz in the first years after my mother's death. If I had stayed in the city with my family, things would have been much harder for me, despite the fact that my father and brothers adjusted so well. Still, a tragedy had occurred and they had gone through a crisis. I don't believe that my father could have taken care of me by himself and my brothers were too young. The kibbutz was the best possible place for me then. I was with relatives who became my foster-family. I knew them and loved them and I had always enjoyed my visits with them on the kibbutz. My foster parents were very understanding, and I never had the feeling that I was an outsider. I always felt like one of their own children. Also this family was well liked by the other children on the kibbutz. I enjoyed having and being spoiled by two families. In my opinion kibbutz society is a very healthy one for a child who was orphaned to be in.

Question 3

Well, from what I've said, it is clear that the best thing is to send the child to a kibbutz. I don't mean to send the child away and get rid of the problem. I mean only if there is a family on a kibbutz that is willing and able to take the child, a good family and preferably one that the child has met before. At the same time his own family must continue to take care of the child. I think kibbutz society is ideally suited to mitigate the child's suffering and to enhance his chances of readjustment. Here the child doesn't feel different, as he would be in the city, and there are usually other orphans on the kibbutz placed with foster families. In addition, the relationship and contact between children and parents on a kibbutz are not as close as they are in the city. In my opinion and based on my experience, the kibbutz is a wonderful place to raise children, especially children who have been through a tragedy. However, each case should be considered individually. It is important that the family which takes the child will be capable of taking care of him, will devote a lot of time and attention to him and will treat him like one of its own children. Also, the child's wishes should be considered.

Question 4

In my opinion, and I think that should be obvious, the fact of a parent's death must not be concealed from a child. Neither must notification of the death be delayed. Because the longer you put it off, the more you hesitate and the more difficult it becomes to tell the truth. It is better to tell the child immediately, to tell him everything, and to answer his questions (if he asks) frankly. Nothing should be concealed, because it will be much harder on the child to learn the truth from other sources. As for the age at which a child should be told, I think it will vary from one case to another. It depends on the circumstances of the parent's death, on whether the child has had any prior preparation, on whether anyone has ever talked to him about death before, etc. In principle, the child should be told no matter what his age. If the child is too young to understand the word 'died' for instance, he can be told 'has gone away and will never return'. The child should get an explanation, in terms that he can understand, of how his parent died, of what causes, and of the significance of the parent's death for the child. This can be explained to a child of any age, on his level of understanding. Even if the adult who does the explaining is not certain that the child is capable of grasping the significance of what he is told, he should still be told. He should be encouraged to ask questions and made to feel that anything he doesn't understand will be explained again.

Now as to my own case. My case was somewhat special because I more or less understood, in the months before her death, that her condition was serious. Of course I didn't think that she would die.

156

But in the half year period preceding her death, while I lived on the kibbutz, I accepted the fact of being parted from her. During all this period I saw her only once. After that I was told that she was so ill that no one could visit her. I accepted that. As for the notification, one morning my foster father came to me with a very sad face (I still remember the scene clearly) and said, "I want to tell you something sad... your mother has died", and then we were both silent. I didn't cry, though I think I understood what he had said. I understood I'd never see my mother again. After a few minutes he told me that she had died at the hospital several hours before. He asked me if I wanted to ask him any questions and I said no. He told me that my father and brothers were at home and that's about all. Then (perhaps because he saw how quiet I had become) he invited me to come to his workshop and play with anything I wanted. I used to like doing that and it made me feel wonderful. I still remember that I chose the game I liked most. I sat for hours and played. I don't remember thinking special thoughts while playing. I did feel that this day was different from other days. I think that I did not feel any special grief because I had been parted from my mother for half a year and the notification of her death was merely the final confirmation of that parting.

Question 5

As to whether children should be taken to the funeral, I think it depends on circumstances. It depends on the background, the circumstances of the death, and most important, on the child's age. In general, I think that the child should be asked if he wants to go, if he is old enough to grasp the significance of the situation. He must not be forced to go. If he doesn't express the wish to go, it can be suggested to him. As to age, I think children under 6 years of age should not be taken. It could be a shock the child will not recover from all his life. If a child does attend the funeral he should be individually accompanied by an adult who will explain exactly what is happening, so that the child is not left wondering about things he doesn't understand, because such things may lead to misconceptions and even nightmares. If an older child, say 11, is afraid of attending the funeral, he should be encouraged to go, he should get an explanation of why it is important for him to go, and he should be told exactly what happens at the funeral. I think that the funeral helps the child to understand what has happened. Things become more clear. The child sees with his own eyes that his father or mother is being buried. It is important for him to see it for himself.

I was six years old (actually it was a few months before my 6th birthday). No one spoke to me about the funeral and no one suggested that I go. I am still sorry about that. First, there was the distance. The kibbutz was very far from the city. Second, I was already emotionally detached from my mother. However, I think I should have been taken to the funeral. I should not have been asked if I wanted to go because such a choice would have confused me. On one hand, I think I would have been very scared of the occasion, but on the other hand I would have been embarrassed to say I didn't want to go. Also, I think I would have wanted to go.

Question 6

A child should be taken to visit the gravesite of his deceased parent. The age at which he is taken depends on the child and on his wish to go. At no age should a child be forced to go. If he refuses to go, an effort can be made to persuade him by explanation. I think if a child has not been to his parent's grave by the time he is 13, he should be strongly encouraged to go, at least once a year, for memorial services. I went for the first time when I was 13. I may have been once before but I don't remember. Anyway, when I went I was with my whole family – father, brothers, aunts and uncles. Since years had passed from the time of my mother's death and the grief was not 'fresh', what was said to me on that occasion was not so relevant. By then I was old enough to understand the significance of death fully. From then on I joined my family for memorial services every year. Then I was living with my family and it was taken for granted that I would go with the others.

In the case of a younger child, it is important to explain to him what he sees and what is happening. He should be in the company of his close family and someone should be at his disposal to answer questions, provide explanations and listen to the expression of his feelings.

Question 7

I think the child should stay home during the Shiv'a, he should see that nothing is being concealed from him, that nothing terrible is happening. He shouldn't feel that in addition to being parted forever from his deceased parent he must also be parted for a while from the other members of his family.

As for me, I stayed on at the kibbutz and continued with my routine. I received no special treatment. Only sometimes I felt that I was being given special consideration and privileges and sometimes I even took advantage of this.

I think that it is very advisable that teachers and classmates come to visit the child during the Shiv'a. I definitely think it helps.

Question 8

My being an orphan made me different from other children in general, but on the kibbutz I felt less different because there were a few more 'cases' like myself. I remember thinking, after I was told my mother was dead, "Today I am different, not like the other children". I expected to be treated differently, to be spoiled, and I took advantage of my position. Not that I expected pity, and I never felt that I was pitied. After I rejoined my family I sometimes saw acquaintances look at me with pity but I don't remember that bothering me. But as I remember it now, it seemed strange that people should pity me because I had accepted being an orphan relatively quickly. My status as an orphan bothered me more when I went to high school. At the kibbutz I had not been so much an exception, because there were others like myself. In the city I was more of an exception and it bothered me. I didn't want to be thought different, and I even sometimes tried to conceal the fact that I was an orphan.

Question 9

I can answer this question but not based on personal experience. Since I stayed on the kibbutz I was not involved in my father's social life. I think that the fact that the widowed parent is seeing someone of the opposite sex should not be kept from his children. I think the parent should explain his situation, his wishes, his feelings, etc. to his children and even ask for their advice in the matter. If the father has been going out with someone for a long time and has serious intentions, he should bring the woman home and introduce her to his children. Then, or even before, he should tell them of his intentions for the future and listen to what they have to say.

As for my case, as I've said before, I was not involved in my father's social life because I was on the kibbutz. As far as I know, he didn't go out in the first years after my mother's death and devoted himself to my brothers and me. When I was about 12-13, he met my stepmother. After a while he started bring her occasionally to visit me on the kibbutz. (He used to visit me every weekend and she would join him about once a month.) He never told me of his plans to marry her but I understood that she wasn't just a friend. Some hints were dropped here and there, but there were many hesitations. I knew that they wanted me to live with them after they were married but I wanted to stay on the kibbutz. On the day they were married (it was a short ceremony) they both came to see me. My father took me aside and said "We were married today" and that was it. Then we all went on a trip.

Question 10

Question 11

I was 13 when my father remarried. I don't have a clearcut opinion about remarriage. I think it depends on the situation — on the person your parent marries, on her status, on whether she has children of her own, on what their plans for these children are. In many cases remarriage is helpful for the parent. He again has someone to share his life with, and his children will not, after all, stay with him forever. And a person, especially when he gets older, needs someone to share his life. In some cases the step-parent can also be a substitute, more or less, for the deceased parent. If this is so, the remarriage is advantageous for the child. If it is not so, the remarriage is disadvantageous for the child. It depends on the personality of the step-parent and on the children's willingness to accept him. It also depends on the children's age.

I think when a parent remarries his children need help in adjusting to the situation. It would be preferable for the parent or the step-parent to provide this help, but if such help is not forthcoming from them it could come from the outside. It should be explained to the child how important it is for the parent to remarry, that it is advantageous for the parent and often also for his children. The child must also be helped to understand the position of the step-parent and how difficult it is for him to become responsible for the care and upringing of children that are not his own and who may have made a bad first impression on him. It is difficult for a step-parent to fulfill the role of the deceased parent and he has his own problems.

Question 12

I don't remember any special fears.

Interview of Subject No. 4

The subject is a 16-year-old girl whose father was killed in the army when she was one and a half years old. Her mother has been living with another man for ten years and has a child by him.

Question 1

I was one and a half years old when my father was killed. A baby. I remember almost nothing. I remember always asking my mother to take me 'to that place' (his grave) so that I could help take care of the plants.

My mother is a very nervous person, lately a little less so, but I can never talk to her. I can't do anything with her. I know that if my father had been alive, I could have had fun with him, we could have laughed and been boisterous together. Not with mother. She never has time. If father were alive, he would understand me. Everyone said I look like him − I have his eyes, his face, his hair. Also his character. Father never liked to study, just like me, and he was disorganized, just like me. Mother is very angry with me for being so disorganized, but father would have understood, he wouldn't be making remarks about it all the time.

Question 2

In one of his last letters to mother my father asked her to raise me the way he would have wanted me raised. This gave me a lot of strength. Every year in the summer I used to come to the kibbutz in order to be close to everything that he was close to and loved. Now I am living on the kibbutz and I'm very happy.

Another thing. After my father was killed the kibbutz published a pamphlet in his memory. Through this pamphlet and through my talks with mother I got to know my father and that helped a lot. My only memory of my father is what I learned from that.

Question 3

Talk, talk, talk. My talks with mother helped me a lot. She would tell me what kind of a man he was and what fun they had. We would sit for hours talking and looking at pictures. You have to know that he is dead and will never return but you have to keep talking about him and loving him.

Another thing. No one can take father's place, but the man that my mother is living with has helped me a lot. He used to play with me, we read together, go for walks and take trips together, and we talk a lot. I tell him everything, even more than I tell mother, because I can't always talk to her and I certainly can't be wild with her.

Another thing. The Ministry of Defense makes it a practice to gather all the bereaved families every so often. Last summer all the Bar Mitzvah boys and girls (13-year-olds) went on a trip abroad. It's wonderful to see everybody, to talk and to see how everyone is doing. I write to some of them and I see that I am not the only one having a difficult time.

I would suggest a program of 'big brother' and 'big sister' from among these orphans for younger orphaned children. They were orphaned at a young age themselves and they would be good to talk to, be with and ask advice of.

Question 4

I think the fact of a parent's death should not be concealed from a child. The orphan should be treated the same as the widow – like an adult. Of course, not in the case of babies. But from kindergarten age on, it is possible to tell the child and he should be told, rather than being sent off to his grandmother or to an aunt and being told that his Daddy has gone abroad. The child should be told the whole truth immediately.

When my father was killed I was a year and a half. Of course, I didn't understand anything then. I don't remember at what age I was told but it was at an early age. I remember going to visit the gravesite every day and that I thought it was just a little garden – our garden.

I remember when later my mother showed me the pamphlet that the kibbutz published in my father's memory, that I wanted to look at it all the time and to hear the same stories about my father again and again...

Question 5

I think children should be taken to the funeral. It is very important that the family should be together during difficult moments. The bereaved family should always stay together. The children must not be left at home and the mother must not attend the funeral without them. I think that from the age of about five children can attend the funeral, though it depends on the child. But the child should be told exactly what happens beforehand so that he doesn't get a shock and doesn't begin thinking all kinds of thoughts.

If the child doesn't want to go, he shouldn't be forced, but he should get an explanation of what exactly happens at a funeral and why it is important for his mother, and for himself, that he should attend.

I was not taken to my father's funeral. I was only a baby and didn't understand.

Question 6

I think children should be taken to visit their parent's grave even at a young age and immediately after the tragedy. They should know that their parent is buried there. They should know where their parent is.

I know from what mother has told me that she took me to the gravesite immediately after the tragedy. She would take me out there every day on her bicycle. At first I didn't understand anything and I would ask her to take me out to the 'garden' because we would take care of the plants and water the flowers there. I understood that my father was buried there only a long time afterwards.

Question 7

I think that staying home during the Shiv'a should be up to the child and he shouldn't be pressured. If he wants to stay home, he should, and if he doesn't, he shouldn't. The idea of the Shiv'a seems generaly foolish to me and artificial — at first the house is crowded with people and after the Shiv'a it is empty and deserted. I think that could be very difficult.

The child staying home during the Shiv'a or not does not prove or disprove his love for his deceased parent. It is just an outward form of mourning. It is important for people to visit the bereaved family, but not just during the Shiv'a.

I was just a baby in the nursery at that time.

Question 8

I was different from other children — I didn't have a father. I don't have a father now, and I remain different. In the past mother and I were very much alone, but now we have the man my mother is living with. He is not my father but he makes a big difference. I don't remember children making things hard on me or helping me. They would sometimes ask about my father and I would tell them.

Question 9

I think men should come to visit the widow. Not many men, just some of father's friends, close friends, or a boy friend of hers. A man's presence is important for the atmosphere at home, for the widow and for the children.

It is also advisable for the widow to remarry. Her remarrying doesn't mean that she has forgotten her first husband. But she should consider her children's wishes because her remarriage will affect their lives too.

Question 10

It was very difficult for me. We were always alone. My mother was always sad, nervous and angry. Since she has been living with her man-friend everything has changed for the better.

Question 11

I think it is to the orphan's advantage that his mother remarry. It is the healthy thing to do — there is a man in the house, the woman is no longer alone and she has someone with whom to share her responsibilities and problems. So she is less moody and depressed. On the other hand, it might be difficult for the child if his mother stops paying attention to him, or if she forgets his father.

I — that is, we — have a 'man of the house'. Mother married him when I was 7 and I even have a little brother. My new father brought happiness to our house. Mother is very happy with him and he is a charming person. He has changed the atmosphere in our home. But neither I nor my mother have forgotten my father.

Question 12

I don't remember any special fears.

Interview of Subject No. 5

The subject is 28 years old. He has a high school education. He lost his father when he was 17.

Question 1

First and foremost was the sense of emptiness, the physical absence. You sit down at the table and father isn't there. It took me a long time to grasp that, and actually I haven't accepted it yet, emotionally.

There are a number of things that I found very hard. For instance, seeing my mother walk through the room holding father's eyeglasses and then throwing them into the trash can. I considered her almost a murderess then.

During the Shiv'a I was bothered by the unnatural manner in which people behaved — everyone whispering, etc. I remember a child (some relative) coming up to me and asking if my father was dead and all my aunts pouncing on him angrily. I didn't mind answering the child.

It bothered me that I hadn't attended the funeral (because it was held before I returned from abroad). It bothered me that I wasn't really allowed to mourn in my own way. When I returned from abroad and entered the house I found everyone sitting Shiv'a. I couldn't speak and began to cry but everyone immediately began trying to calm me down. I remember thinking that I wasn't even crying loudly and wondering why they wouldn't let me cry. It also bothered me that no one told me exactly how and when my father died.

Question 2

The Shiv'a for me was actually a number of social gatherings in which I talked about my trip to the U.S. I was very glad that many friends came and I appreciated the fact that those who weren't close friends came too. These social evenings seemed natural. What made the Shiv'a hard on me were the regular prayers that were observed. I needed to be alone. One time I locked myself in my room and listened to music. It was great.

Question 3

My suggestion is that when a child or adolescent is orphaned he should be allowed to feel and do whatever he wants to. He should be allowed to express his feelings and given the freedom to mourn in his own way.

Widows should be advised not to conceal their true feelings from their children. Not to play act. But the mother should try to be strong and continue to function. If there are economic difficulties, she should not tell the child, she should even hide them from him. For example, if they have to move to a smaller apartment she shouldn't tell the child that it is because they can't afford to keep their present one. She could say it is because the present one reminds her too much of her husband, etc. If the child is made aware of the lack of money (and money is something intangible for a child) he may develop fears, and be afraid of asking for things.

Question 4

The child ought to be told that his father is dead and not that he has gone away. At any age when the child is already capable of understanding, he should be told that his father is dead. If he doesn't understand and asks what dead means, it can be explained to him by means of previous experiences he may have had with dead animals, etc. Since children are curious, they will probably ask questions, and then they can be given explanations.

As for me, my father died when I was abroad. I received a telephone message to return home immediately, and I immediately understood that father had died, because he had been very ill. But I was not actually told on the telephone that he was dead. When I came home two days later, I was not told exactly what had happened either. Until this day I don't know exactly how he died and I think that's bad. When I got the message abroad I knew he was dead and yet I hoped that I might see him once more. Seeing him would have helped me to accept the situation. As soon as I got the message I began to cry. When I returned home I began to cry again, but everyone tried to stop me from crying.

Question 5

It is important to be at the funeral because it helps you to accept the cruel truth. It is important as a parting. Small children should not be forced to go to the funeral. The child should be asked if he wants to go, no matter what age he is. It is important that someone be with him, and perhaps prevent him from seeing the painful part. But it is important for the child to be there, to remember having been there.

I was not present at my father's funeral because I was abroad. They told me later that the Rabbinate did not agree to delay the funeral till I returned. But I still feel guilty about not having been to the funeral. I find it hard to accept the fact of his death psychologically because I didn't see him buried. Several weeks after the funeral someone remarked, "It's a good thing you weren't at the funeral, because you are very sensitive" and ever since then I have thought that maybe they could have waited for me to return and deliberately didn't.

Question 6

I saw my father's grave for the first time after the Shiv'a. I was afraid of seeing it and surprised that there was no tombstone yet. The first time in my life I had ever seen a grave was when I was in eighth grade and mother took me to see grandma's grave. I was very scared to go but afterwards I felt relieved and very grown up.

Question 7

As to the Shiv'a, children, like adults, should be allowed to decide what they want to do. If they want to stay home, they should, and if they want to go to school, they should. The main thing is that the child be allowed to decide and not forced.

I was a high school student when my father died. The school principal called up and said he was shocked to hear of our tragedy. He was sorry he couldn't come because it was so difficult to reach our house by bus. I was hurt, because it was possible to reach our house by bus. It made me very angry. No teachers came. Some classmates came, but not the whole class. I suppose they were afraid. In my opinion teachers and all classmates should come to visit the bereaved child during the Shiv'a. Seeing the people with whom he normally has daily contact will convey a sense of continuity and the thought that life must go on.

The friends who did come did not talk about death and I did not get any emotional support from them. I think it is very important to get such support from teachers and friends. Physical presence alone is not enough. There should be emotional support through talk about the deceased — the orphan should be asked how his parent died, how he feels, etc.

Question 8

Yes, I thought I was different. I felt I had aged, grown up before my time. Now I realize how much I missed a father figure. Maybe then I didn't realize it. I used to envy my cousins, who when they needed money simply had to ask their father for it. Some of them also work with their fathers. I'll never be able to do that.

Friends neither made things difficult nor helped. They didn't know exactly what to do. I don't know whether friends can help at all. I remember a saying: "Don't tell your friends your troubles, because half of them don't care, and the other half will be glad to hear of them...".

Question 9

No matter what their age, a mother should share her plans and feelings about her boy friend with her children. She probably has some doubts and she should share them with her children. As to remarriage, I think the children should be allowed to express their opinion, but in the end the mother must do what she considers best. Even if the child objects. I mean, there is a gamble involved, but it usually pays off and the child will eventually accept the situation (unless there is hatred between mother and child). In the final analysis the decision is the mother's because everyone must live his own life.

As for me, I didn't even know that my mother had a boy friend. I was serving in the army and once when I came home unexpectedly I found him there. They pretended they were just friends and had met by chance and my mother said to him "Perhaps you'd like to come to dinner tomorrow?", but I knew they were pretending. I think such behavior stems from ignorance. My mother was apparently afraid of my reaction so she kept it from me.

I understood that they wanted to get married and were afraid of my reaction so I said that I wanted to move out of the house and into an apartment of my own. Then they finally spoke to me about it, but even then they didn't come right out and say they wanted to get married. My mother's boy friend said to me jokingly "Do you mind if I take your mother with me for a while?"

Question 10

My mother made things harder for me. First of all, she never cried in front of me. Whenever she felt like crying she would run into her bedroom, close the door and cry there. I didn't know what to do. I didn't know whether I should go to her or not. It seemed inhuman. That was the hardest of all. That hardship was caused by mother indirectly. She also caused me hardship directly. She would tell me of our financial trouble, of the income tax we had to pay, and that frightened me terribly. I thought maybe I shouldn't ask for new clothes. Actually things were not so bad but mother gave me the feeling they were. I think the widow must recognize the fact that after her husband's death the financial problems of the family are hers to handle and she should not burden her children with them.

Question 11

I don't think a widow should refrain from remarrying because of her children. It is her duty to take care of her children and to do what's best for them. And what is best for them is that she should remarry and be happy, so that they need not worry about her on that account.

The first thing that must be explained to the child is that the man his mother marries will not take the place of his father and will not cause him to be forgotten. He must understand that life must go on. The best thing is for his stepfather to say these things to the child.

Question 12

Before my father's death I don't recall having fears, but after he died I felt certain feelings, I don't know whether to describe them as fear or as guilt. I am still afraid that I may have been wrong to leave my father ill and to go on a trip abroad. I feel guilty about missing his funeral. It is important to reassure a person that he didn't act wrongly.

Subject No. 6

The subject is 30 years old and lost her mother when she was 11. She has a high school education and is a mother to two children.

Question 1

The thing that was the hardest for me was that we never spoke of mother. There was a terrible silence. For many years (until I was 26) I couldn't pronounce the word mother. Not until I grew up and underwent group therapy. The problem was that for many years I knew no details about her death. She had been ill for a week and was taken to the hospital suddenly. I only recently found out that my aunt came to visit my mother, saw that her condition was serious and took her to the hospital. Now I know that she was suffering from a serious abdominal illness. I was told that my mother had been taken to the hospital to give birth. She was pregnant. Before mother became ill, she had made me a pretty white dress which I still remember. She even ironed it. She told me that after she will have the baby I should put on that dress to come and visit her at the hospital. The day after she was taken to the hospital my aunt came to our house. I had been told that mother had given birth and I didn't understand why my aunt wasn't happy. My aunt wasn't happy. My aunt told me that my mother passed away and I didn't even understand the words 'passed away'. I was confused and I couldn't understand why every one was so sad and why I was not dressed in my pretty new white dress when I was taken to the hospital. I understood that something terrible had happened from the oppressive atmosphere, but nobody told me clearly and directly what had happened. I was not allowed to go to the funeral. I don't remember what happened afterwards. For years after that no one spoke to me about mother or about what happened to her.

Because we didn't speak about mother I couldn't think about her either. I felt that if it was wrong to speak of her, it must be wrong to think of her. But I missed her terribly in the first year, and I cried a lot. Everything seemed to be back to normal and it was very difficult. At the age of 26, after having undergone group therapy, I asked my brother to come over and for the first time in 15 years, we talked about our mother. It was an experience that I and my brother will never forget.

Question 2

What helped to make things a bit easier for me was the fact that after two years I came to live on a kibbutz and that helped me to recover somewhat. My brother was there too and father used to visit us regularly every week or two. But no one on the kibbutz talked to me about the painful subject either, and that is a pity.

Question 3

First of all I would advise talking to the child and explaining exactly what happened. When my father died four years ago, and we sat Shiv'a, I felt much better. I was already in therapy and I was no longer afraid to talk about the subject. For a whole week my brother and I talked of nothing but father and we relived our life with him in that way. It was very helpful and made the pain more bearable. It enabled me to go back to normal life without being burdened by his death.

Question 4

I think that the person closest to the child should tell him the truth even if this is difficult. If the person closest to the child finds it impossible to tell him, someone else should do it, but it must be someone close to the child.

I think a child should be told everything, immediately, no matter what his age. I was notified by my aunt that my mother had passed away. I didn't understand what she was telling me because I didn't

174

understand the expression 'passed away'. By my aunt's behavior I could tell that something had happened to my mother, but I didn't understand exactly what because I had been told that she was taken to hospital to have a baby. I don't remember how I reacted, I just remember that my aunt came and told me and that I didn't understand what she was saying.

Question 5

It's hard for me to say whether children should be taken to the funeral. I'm not sure. I'm certain that they shouldn't be forced to go. From a certain age I think it should be suggested that the child should go, below a certain age it might be traumatic. Perhaps the age should be 6. Certain families, from the Oriental community for instance, have very noisy demonstrative funerals and that might be traumatic for a child. On the other hand, despite it being a very difficult experience, it allows one to express grief instead of repressing it.

I don't remember whether I was given the choice of going to the funeral or not. I remember being taken to the hospital before the funeral and after that I don't remember anything. But I'm sure I wasn't taken to the funeral. As I think of it and as I feel even now, I am very sorry that I was not at my mother's funeral.

Question 6

In my opinion children should be taken for a visit to the cemetery no matter what their age. When the child is taken depends on the family. The child should be taken when the adult who takes him feels strong enough. I think after the Shiv'a, after everyone is somewhat recovered. It depends on the occasion. I don't remember when I first went. Almost everything associated with my mother's death has been blocked out from my memory. I don't remember anything. I think I first went after the mourning. I remember that some relatives came from the United States and that I was at the cemetery with them but I don't remember how old I was then.

I don't know what advice to give about going to the cemetery. It depends on the case. In some cases it would be preferable that the surviving parent should take the child, and in other cases someone who is not as emotionally involved. The child should be told the truth so that he can begin dealing with it. He should not be spoken to in euphemisms, as I was.

Question 7

In my opinion the child should stay home during the Shiv'a. I stayed home with all my family. This is a chance for the child to release some of his tension, and to begin to understand what has happened. My mother died a few days before summer vacation began. I don't think my teacher came to visit me. I remember that it was very hard for me to return to school at the beginning of the next year. I didn't know whether the other children knew and how they would react. No children in the class had come to visit me because the Shiv'a was during the summer vacation. Children from the neighborhood did come. I definitely think it's important that the teacher should visit. It helps the orphan to maintain contact with his class so that it is later easier for him to return to school without the problems of wondering who knows and what they know. The home-room teacher can prepare the class and guide them in how to behave with the orphan so as not to hurt his feelings.

Question 8

I remember being afraid of what the other children would say and of the questions they might ask, but I don't remember how they actually reacted. I remember my brother's reaction to other children's imprecations that included the word 'mother'. He would go wild, beat up the child who uttered the imprecation and then start crying hysterically because they had 'cursed his mother'. The children in the neighborhood knew that we were orphans and I don't think they ever did it deliberately, but in the heat of an argument they sometimes forgot.

176

I think I am different from other people because I was orphaned. I am convinced that the fact that I didn't have a mother when I was going through adolescence has affected my personality. I needed professional treatment and it has helped me. I think I lacked a mother-figure to identify with.

Question 9

I think a widower can definitely bring women home, as long as he doesn't bring a different woman every day. If he has serious intentions about a woman he should bring her home. It doesn't pay to conceal a relationship with a woman or plans to remarry from children. My father didn't remarry for a long time and he didn't bring girl friends home. I think he was afraid it would hurt us. Only when I was 17 and both my brother and I were on the kibbutz did father talk to us about his girl friend. He asked for our opinion. We encouraged him to marry. Only then did he take us to meet her. I don't think children should be asked for their opinion on the matter, though it made me feel good when father asked us.

Question 10

The fact that father was a widower wasn't particularly hard on us. It was not his widowhood, but rather the lack of our mother that was hard. Father was very devoted to us and we were close. Although he worked very hard and it was difficult for him, he never neglected us. We had a woman to take care of us till he returned from work. When I was 17 father remarried. Since I was on the kibbutz, the term step-mother was of less significance to me.

Question 11

— — — — —

177

Question 12

I sometimes have the fear of dying like my mother. It is interesting that when I was a child I didn't have that fear but as an adult, during my pregnancy, I was afraid that my mother's case would repeat itself. And this fear appeared at the time when I was already able to talk about my mother and I had learned not to repress things. Perhaps because I was married and had my first baby at the same age my mother was married and had her first baby.

Interview of Subject No. 7

The subject is 18 years old. Her father died suddenly when she was 11.

Question 1

The main hardship lay in the fact that because of my being an orphan I was given too much freedom, and that also meant too much responsibility. I could do almost whatever I wanted, and this sometimes led me into situations which I knew were bad for me.

About a year and a half ago I started seeing a psychologist. I made the decision to see her. When I started treatment I consciously transferred all responsibility to my psychologist. That felt very good. Now I had someone to set the limits for me, to take care of me.

Question 2

In the evening (I learned of my father's death in the morning) my teacher came to the house and talked to me about father (she had known him). We had a very intimate chat, and she told me about her own tragedy — she had lost her daughter.

Her visit came just at the right time. People had come to be with my mother and my older sister's friends were there and I was alone. When my teacher came in I started crying. Afterwards, through all the years of school I felt I had a special relationship with that teacher.

Another thing that helped me was a wonderful relationship I had with my father. I was his favorite daughter and we had made each other happy.

Question 3

I would suggest that people who have experienced a personal tragedy themselves should talk to orphans. Talking to such a person would give the orphan the feeling of being understood.

Question 4

I think the child should be informed of the death immediately, no matter what his age. As soon as the child learns of the death, the details don't matter much. Later he can be given all the details. In some cases the details might stimulate the child's imagination and that might be harmful, but that can't be foreseen. Now as I am speaking of my father's death, for example, I can clearly see the room he was in, the bed, etc. – although I wasn't there.

I was notified by my mother. I was sitting with my sister, eating. My mother came in and said, "Father's dead". My sister became hysterical and began screaming and rolling on the floor. Mother hugged her and they cried on the floor together. I remained sitting at the table, dazed by what I had heard and by my sister's hysterical behavior. Later my mother told us the details.

Question 5

I think children should be taken to the funeral no matter what their age. I don't think they should be asked. They should be made to feel that there is no possibility of not going. It was clear to me and to my sister that we would attend the funeral.

The funeral helped me to understand the finality of death. I saw my father being lowered into the ground and covered over and I understood he was with us no longer. I think seeing the burial prevents the child from developing fantasies about it.

I remember the whole funeral. I particularly remember the togetherness, my mother, sister and I, holding on to each other. It was important to me that so many people came to the funeral (and to the memorial services).

During the last memorial service held for father I became interested, for the first time, in the content of the service and I read the psalms that were part of the service and tried to understand them. Also at the same memorial service one of my relatives was tidying around the grave and I remember feeling hurt, feeling that it was 'mine' and no one had a right to do that but me.

Question 6

My mother goes to the cemetery once every two weeks, to water the plants and tidy the gravesite. I also go there often, usually when I'm in a bad mood and want to 'talk' to father. I feel at home there, I feel I can do whatever I want. The last time I was there was on a Saturday and the caretaker told me that it isn't proper to visit a cemetery on a Saturday but I felt that I had a right to visit 'my' grave any time I wanted, no matter what the religious practice was.

Question 7

We did not observe the Shiv'a. The first evening after the funeral my teacher came and talked to me about my father (she had known him), about things of an intimate nature, and about her losing her own daughter. On the third day my teacher came with my whole class and then they took me to school with them. It was the most natural thing to do because my mother had also returned to work.

I never thought about observing Shiv'a but now that I'm asked about it, I think it might be a good idea. If I had observed the full week of mourning, things might have been different for me at school and I might not have expected so much pity and attention.

The visit of the teacher and the children in the orphan's class help the orphan in returning to school, so I strongly recommend such visits. I myself went to visit a child who was orphaned a few months after my father died and I believe my visit helped him even if I didn't say very much.

Question 8

I didn't feel different in a negative sense. I even felt somehow superior. But I did feel different. Now I feel a sense of kinship with other orphans more than I feel different from people who have both parents. It is good to feel that there are others who share my fate. My mother has given me a lot of love, enough for five mothers and fathers.

Other children helped. They pitied me and I wanted their pity. The first birthday I had after my father's death, the children surprised me with a party and a beautiful gift. I became very popular and took part in many activities. I don't know if my popularity stemmed from pity or from the fact that I had perhaps become more sociable and active.

Question 9

On this subject things between my mother and my sister and me were pretty much out in the open. We knew what was going on though we didn't talk about it much. My sister suggested that mother join a group of widowed parents.

At first it was clear that no one could take father's place, because no one could be like him (as a husband). Later on mother wanted to remarry and looked for the right man. When one of these men was not to my liking I would make it clear to mother and often when he would come in I would leave the house. Now I know it wasn't very nice of me.

Then my mother met this man. We talked about him moving in with us. I thought, if I got along with him, fine; if I didn't, I would move out. Anyway, for me he will remain my mother's husband. I think he will always be a guest, an outsider. My sister and I like him and feel free with him and he brings us a lot of presents.

I think the children should be consulted before their mother remarries. If the children don't like their mother's husband there are bound to be problems.

It is not always advisable to remarry. For instance, if the widow is an older woman, sex is no longer so important, and if she is able to keep busy, there is no reason she should get married.

Question 10

When both my sister and I go out, we try to arrange for one of us to get back early so that my mother isn't alone. It bothers me that my mother has to deal with everything by herself, and I can't help her. If my father were alive, some of the problems she has to deal with wouldn't even exist. Sometimes, when I am the one causing the problems I say to myself, "Stop, you have a mother who has to deal with everything alone." My mother keeps busy, she works and is active in various groups, although that requires a lot of self-discipline.

Question 11

I find it hard to talk about the advantages and disadvanages of having a step-father. If the child is bothered by having only one parent then his parent's remarriage can make him more like other children, at least superficially. But I don't feel that way.

I also have my own ideas about bringing men home. I'm not sure it's good for every family. I myself am against the possibility of a new father, of 'a man in the house' because I think every child chooses a father figure for himself (sometimes even his dead father) and there is no sense in forcing a new father figure on him.

Question 12

I was afraid that my mother would die and of what would happen to me if she died. I became hysterical because of that fear only once. Once when I returned from a trip my mother and sister were not at home. I sat outside waiting for them and worrying, and imagining various possibilities of what could have happened to them. I thought of accidents and death until I began to cry. After a while my sister called and said not to worry. They had really been involved in an accident but were unhurt and were on their way home.

I worry about my mother when she's ill or doesn't feel so well but I no longer get panicky, and for example, I don't put pressure on her to see a doctor.

Interview of Subject No. 8

The subject is 26 years old and a student at the university. He lost his mother when he was 7 and his father when he was 24.

Question 1

I don't remember any special hardships, maybe because I was raised by my aunt.

Immediately after my mother died I went to live with my aunt (who wasn't married and who had no children of her own), and my father used to come to see me every day, but he didn't live with us. This arrangement continued until I was 15.

My aunt was like a mother to me, and took care of all my needs, so I had a mother image. My father, though he was not in good health and worked very hard, was also always there for me. Actually I really began to feel an orphan when my father died. At that time I was completely independent, I had been living with my father and helping to support him (ever since I remember myself I have been working), and when he died I felt I was completely alone.

I have no painful memories connected with mother's death which disturb me, but I think I still haven't gotten over my father's death, though it's been two years.

Question 2

The main thing is the continuation of the family framework. I think my aunt's care was the main thing that helped me to adjust and develop.

What helped me most after my father's death was that I was independent and self supporting. I was strongly affected by his death but I wasn't broken. I continued with my life. I think my independence gave me strength.

Another thing that helped me after my father's death was going to the synagogue. I went every day for a year and I felt it strengthened me.

Question 3

I think the best thing is to find someone in the family to take care of the child until he reaches an age when he no longer needs constant care. Someone who can take the mother's place, give the child a sense of family, and serve as a mother-figure.

Question 4

I think the death should not be concealed from a child. People think that children don't understand and sense things, but they do, and it is wrong to deceive them.

Notification of death need not include all the painful details. It should be clear and simple so that the child understands, but he should not be burdened with details which will make it more painful for him, such as how many hours his parent suffered on his death-bed, etc.

In my case, neither of my parents died suddenly. Each died after a long illness and hospitalization.

I don't remember so many details in connection with my mother's death but I remember that when I was notified I had a clear sense of her death. My mother had cancer and she suffered greatly before her death. She was very ill for a year before she died and the last two months she was in the hospital. That's when I went to live with my aunt. My aunt was the one who notified me of my mother's death. My father was in no condition to do it. He was hardly able to speak. He himself was in bad health for years.

I don't remember exactly what words my aunt used. I think she said "Your mother is gone". I already knew that something was wrong because my father had been brought to my aunt's house in a terrible state and she was taking care of him. However, throughout my mother's illness I never thought of the possibility of her dying and I was sure she would recover. I guess I was just a child and I didn't want to believe in the possibility of death. My aunt was crying when she told me. I didn't cry and it bothered me that I couldn't cry, but when I heard my father's heart-rending sobs I too burst into tears, and, with my aunt hugging me, the three of us cried.

When my father died it was different. I was twenty-four and I had been playing the role of my father's 'father' for a long time. My father had been ill for many years, and for several days before his death he was unconscious. This time I knew the end was near, but I was the one in charge. I had no illusions this time. I was notified by his doctor – cold and clear: "Your father died at five o'clock". I was expecting this, and I didn't cry. I took care of all the funeral arrangements, etc. Then I went to my aunt's and there I broke down and cried.

Question 5

I think children should be taken to the funeral so that the child should not feel that he has betrayed his parent by being absent from his funeral, by not parting from him properly. He also should not be allowed to feel that he was left behind. As for age, at whatever age the child can understand. The child's going to the funeral should be taken for granted but he should be prepared beforehand. It shouldn't seem like some terrible thing to the child, but something natural, part of dying. I didn't attend my mother's funeral because that's what my family decided and I did not object to their decision. I wasn't consulted about it. I was left with relatives. For a long time afterwards I used to dream that my mother wasn't dead and came back to say goodbye to me. I think a child should know what a funeral and a burial really are. He shouldn't be shut out and left to feel that he has betrayed his mother and not parted from her properly. I wasn't even given a chance to say goodbye.

Question 6

Of course children should be taken to the cemetery to visit the gravesite. They have to have something tangible associated with the deceased and not just some insubstantial idea that he is buried. A child should see the grave.

I saw my mother's grave for the first time when I was 9. I asked to be taken. My father wouldn't take me so I went with my aunt. I remember being astonished at the size of the cemetery, at seeing so many graves, at how many dead people there were. When I saw the grave I didn't feel that my mother was buried there. I felt a sense of her being there only after my father died and I went to visit her grave after his funeral.

The fact that I couldn't associate the grave with my mother disturbed me. I think a child should see the grave right after the death to prevent such a sense of estrangement.

Question 7

I think the child should be consulted. If he wants to stay home he should be kept home, and if he wants to return to school he should be allowed to return.

In any case, the child must not feel that things are being concealed from him or that his family wants to get rid of him. He should feel part of the family.

I stayed home with my father and aunt and I think it was a good thing I did. I can't remember whether my teacher came, but I remember that my friends did and at first they were very embarrassed. After a while the ice was broken and we talked naturally about all kinds of things. Finally we also talked about death and that helped me.

I think it is very important that people come to visit during the Shiv'a, particularly friends, because it makes you feel that people care and it helps to take your mind off your grief. You hear people talking about other things and you find that life goes on.

Question 8

I always considered myself different — more grown up, more serious, and less involved in silly, childish things. I did have my aunt to look after me but I felt more grown up.

Question 9

I find it hard to answer this question because personally I have no experience in the matter. There were no women in my father's life. He was always ill, and didn't go out. Besides, I was living with my aunt and not with him.

I think in general such relationships should be carried on outside of the house but their existence should not be concealed from the children. If it comes to remarriage, the parent alone should decide, and his decision should be conveyed to the children together with an explanation.

Question 10

Since a normal family consists of two parents, obviously the fact of my father being a widower bothered me, even though I was living with my aunt. My father was not in good health and I was always worried about his health and about his financial situation. Still, maybe these are not things characteristic of every widower. My father never made any special demands on me, but the fact that he was ill and alone bothered me, even though I wasn't living with him.

Question 11

I think remarriage is good for the orphan because it again establishes a normal family for him and that is a good solution to his problem. A child needs both a father and a mother. The advantage of remarriage is that it returns the child to normal family life. The disadvantage is that a step-parent can never really take the place of the parent.

Question 12

I was mainly afraid about my father. Since he had been ill for years, I was afraid he'd die and I would be left alone. That is why I started working at a very young age, together with going to school. I wanted to be self supporting in case anything happened to my father. What helped me overcome my fears about my father was becoming financially self sufficient and taking over the role of 'father' to my father — taking care of him financially and otherwise.

Interview of Subject No. 9

The subject is 22 and a student at the university. She lost her mother at the age of 11.

Question 1

What was particularly hard for me was the way I was treated by others and my fear of being considered strange and different.

Another thing that was difficult was the burden of the household and the hard work I had to do. Also, shopping for myself and things like that.

Question 2

What helped me most was my immediate family. My father, my brother, and other close relatives. Another thing that helped was the fact that two years after I lost my mother two of my good friends were also orphaned, and that encouraged an openness on my part and a willingness to talk about being an orphan. We talked a lot about the subject and that helped a lot.

Even before my mother died I had been very close to father. He showed me a lot of love and pampered me. He was even more loving after my mother's death and that helped me.

Question 3

An orphan must be helped to understand that he is not exceptional, not different. He should be helped to deal with people's pity on one hand and their withdrawal on the other. People find bereavement hard to deal with. The orphan should also be helped to talk about his situation and feelings.

Question 4

The child should be informed as soon as possible. How he is informed depends on his age. It is advisable that the surviving parent should be the one to inform the child.

My mother had been ill a long time so I had had a time of preparation. I knew she was about to die. I was staying with my aunt, and when she died my father and brother came to my aunt's and told me. I didn't cry much, because I had been prepared for the news. The others didn't cry much either. We had all known it was coming.

Question 5

The child should be taken to the funeral if he is grown up enough, not necessarily chronologically but emotionally. It should be suggested that he attend the funeral but he should not be forced to.

I didn't want to go but my father persuaded me to and I went. I am grateful to him for it because it is important to me to have attended the funeral.

I think some prior preparation on the subject of death is very important for the child. I myself had been prepared, we had talked about death and it was explained to me. This helped me at the funeral because I wasn't surprised. I knew what to expect.

Question 6

I think children should be taken to the cemetery to visit the grave, but again, it depends on the child's maturity and on the preparation he receives.

I went to visit the grave on the 30th day of her death, and on all the subsequent anniversaries of her death. I always went with my father, brother, and other close relatives. We didn't talk much. We just went.

Question 7

I think the child should not go to school during the Shiv'a, unless he absolutely insists on it. I stayed home. My teacher came to visit, but because I didn't think very highly of her, her visit didn't mean much to me. Actually, when I think about it now, I expected her to come and I would have been hurt if she hadn't. My teacher didn't talk to me about my mother or the situation resulting from her death. It was a sort of courtesy visit.

The children in my class came to visit. I think classmates' visits are important because they help to relieve the ennui of the Shiv'a and also because it gives the orphan the feeling that everyone knows of his tragedy and it is not a secret.

Question 8

I felt more mature than my girl friends. I felt this for about 3-4 years after my mother's death. I also was afraid of my father dying. After a while the fear passed. My friends did not worry about their parents.

Question 9

My father didn't bring women to the house. I think that if the parent had a serious relationship with a person of the opposite sex, he should bring that person home. The relationship should not be concealed from the children. I don't think the parent should consult his children remarrying, but he should prepare them for it by explaining why he is doing it and what effect it will have on their life in the future.

Personally, I have always wanted my father to remarry. I think he would have gotten more out of life if he had, and been happier.

Question 10

Having a widower for a father was hard, because he made great demands upon me in the housework and didn't realize what it was doing to me. After a while he understood me better and also, I got used to his demands and adjusted to them better.

I think if my father had received any counseling, I would have been spared a lot of suffering, because he was not aware that he demanded too much of me.

Question 11

I think his parent's remarriage is advantageous to the orphan. First, because it makes the parent a happier person, and second, because it removes some duties and responsibilities from the orphan. It is important that the orphan get to know his step-parent before the remarriage, and if they get along well and like each other, it makes things much easier.

Question 12

After my mother died I was afraid my father and other close members of my family would die too and leave me all alone. I worried about father having an accident while driving but I got over that fear and today I drive too.

Part Six

THE QUESTIONNAIRE: ITS PSYCHOMETRIC CHARACTERISTICS; ADMINISTRATION AND SCORING METHOD; QUANTITATIVE AND QUALITATIVE ANALYSIS AND DIAGNOSIS

1. Questionnaire for Examination of Human and Animal Death Conceptualization of Children Aged 4-12 years.

Sara Smilansky

Name of Child_____Age_____Sex_____
This child lost father/mother by death? Yes No (if yes) How old was he?_____ Examiners Name _____Date _____

Child's Concepts Related to Human Death

1. What does "to die" mean? What is death?_____
   _____

2. Of what do people die? Of what other reasons can people die?
   _____

3. Who gets old? Does everyone get old? (If the child answers "no," ask who does get old?)_____

4. What happens to a person who dies? What do we do with him?
   _____

5. Does a dead person know that he is dead? Does he know what is happening to him? Why? (Ask the child to explain "Why?" if he answers that the dead person does know or that he does not know) _____

   _____

6. Is a dead person able to feel? Does he feel pain? Why _____
   _____

7. If a person dies and has been in his grave for some time, can he return to become a living person? Why? _____

8. If a person dies and has not yet been buried, can he return to become a living person? Why? _____

9. Can a dead person see? Why? _____

10. Can a dead person hear? Why? _____

11. Can a dead person move? Why? _____

12. Can a dead person come out of his grave? Why? _____

_____

13. Does everyone die? Why? (If the child answers "no,", ask who does die?)_____

Child's Concepts Related to Animal Death

14. Have you ever seen a dead cat or dog?_____

15. Of what do cats and dogs die? Of what other reasons can dogs die? If the child's answer to question 14 is that he has seen a dead bird, for instance, include birds in question 15)_____

16. Does a dog get old? Do all dogs get old? (If the answer is "no,", ask which dogs get old?) Why? Do cats get old?_____

_____

17. What do we do with dead dogs and cats?_____

18. Does a dead dog know that he is dead? Why?_____

19. Can a dead dog or a dead cat feel anything? Can he feel pain? Why?_____

20. If a dog dies and is put in the ground, can he become a live dog again? Why? _____

21. If a dog dies and is put into the trash, can he become a live dog again? Why? _____

22. Can a dead dog see? Why? _____

23. Can a dead dog hear? Why? _____

24. Can a dead dog move? Why? _____

25. Can a dead dog get out of wherever he is put? Why? _____

_____

26. Do all dogs die? (If the child answers "no," ask which dogs do die?) _____

_____

_____

_____

_____

_____

_____

_____

2. Rationale Behind the Concepts Selected and Included in the Questionnaire

The "Questionnaire for Examination of Human and Animal Death Conceptualization of Children" contains twenty-six questions relating to various aspects of the death concepts. They deal with the following five concepts: Irreversibility, Finality, Causality, Inevitability, and Old Age. The questions were determined according to two main criteria:

- Significance of understanding each particular concept of death, to a child's mourning process and to his/her readjustment and coping in the new reality.
- Relevant information from research analysis and results from our empirical studies.

Introduction

The loss of a parent is a painful and trying experience for a child, and affects all aspects of his life and personality. The crisis which the child goes through affects his emotional and intellectual development as well as his social relationships. It forces the child to confront the new situation on the emotional as well as the cognitive level. "Mouring" is a psycho-social process, which is composed of various emotional and cognitive processes by means of which the orphan* works through the painful feelings accompanying the tragedy. At the

* In this book the word *orphan* refers to a child who lost his father or mother by death.

197

conclusion of this process the orphan should be able to establish new emotional ties and to function normally in every aspect, considering his potentialities.

A vital precondition for dealing with the new reality is understanding this reality. Coping and readjustment to a reality which has so drastically changed is impossible without cognitive understanding of this reality. The child must have a clear understanding of the fact that his loved one has died and of what death is in general and specifically for him/her.

Although cognitive understanding of death is a vital precondition for mourning, it is not in itself sufficient for readjustment. In addition to understanding, the bereaved child must go through some emotional processes (anger, sadness, fear, etc.). These emotions coupled with adult support and based on cognitive understanding, will help the child to overcome the crisis and to readjust, cope and develop up to his potential. Thus, although cognitive understanding of death is not in itself sufficient for a normal mourning and readjustment process, it is a vital pre-condition in all stages of mourning and readjustment.

We have selected and included in the questionnaire five concepts of death that we found in our empirical study, to correlate highest with the children's achievement in the social, learning and emotional domains. These five death concepts are: 1) Non-reversibility of death, 2) Finality of Death, 3) Causality of death, 4) Inevitability of death, and 5) Old age and death.

A. The Concept of Non-reversibility of Death and its Effect on Mourning and Readjustment of Children

Understanding the concept of non-reversibility involves understanding that death is an irreversible phenomenon which can not be altered. It means understanding that the deceased will never return to be a living person, no matter how passionately we may wish it. Unterstanding this concept also involves relinquishing the deceased as a living person and awareness of our inability to change the biological course of life or turn back biological processes.

The concept of non-reversibility is of major importance at the beginning of the mourning process. The first stage of mourning is, in effect, facing the idea of death's irreversibility. The bereaved child will at first be unwilling to accept, both emotionally and intellectually, that the loved one will never return. Rehabilitation means reorganization of personality, of social relationships, and of habits of life. Such reorganization must take place on the basis of an awareness that reorganization is necessary because there has been a permanent change. Understanding the concept of death's irreversibility is, therefore, the basis for the beginning of the bereaved child's mourning process as well as the basis for the beginning of his/her readjustment. Understanding the concept of non-reversibility does not enable the child automatically the emotional acceptance of non-reversibility but it is a necessary basis for the emotional confrontation and coping.

B. The Concept of Finality of Death and its Effect on Mourning and Readjustment of Children

Understanding the concept of death's finality involves perceiving death as the opposite of life; as a state in which all life's functions cease. In death there is no metabolic function, no motion, no sensation, and no consciousness. To understand death's finality for a child is to understand the fact the the deceased is not alive in any sense of the word 'life'. "The deceased is no longer a person".

The concept of finality affects the first and second stages of mourning as well as the rehabilitation of the bereaved child. Understanding death's finality, like understanding death's irreversibility, helps the child also to accept the very fact of death. Understanding the concept of Finality can also ease the bereaved child's pain, since it will make it clear that the deceased is no longer suffering – the deceased does not feel pain, not hunger, nor cold. When the child understands that he/she need not "worry" about the deceased parent, he/she is more able to concentrate on his/her own grief, thus enabling the child to progress through the mourning process to the readjustment which follows it.

The perception of death's finality will help in the bereaved child's readjustment as well, since it will help the child to understand that the deceased no longer exists *as a living person* and is different in death from what he/she was in life. The child can now gradually learn that he/she need not relate emotionally to the deceased in the same way as before, when the deceased was a living person. This will also enable the child with time to form new emotional attachments, even to a step-father or step-mother without feeling that the deceased is being betrayed.

C. The Concept of Causality of Death and its Effect on Mourning and Readjustment of Children

The concept of death's causality relates to the physical-biological factors which caused the death. The bereaved child must be helped to understand the concept of Causality in general and know, in particular, the causes which led to his deceased parent's death. A child, like any bereaved person, will wonder about what caused the death of the loved one and may feel guilt related to the cause of death. Knowing the causes of death may make things easier. It will help the bereaved child during the second stage of mourning, when anger directed at the deceased, self accusation, and blaming others are very common. Cognitive understanding does not constitute absolute insurance against guilt feelings (based on perception of irrational causes of death). However, *cognitive understanding, together with emotional working through of feelings*, will improve the bereaved child's chances of mourning and of readjustment. When the child is able to perceive the cause of death correctly and to free himself/herself of guilt feelings, he/she will be able to readjust. As long as the child is preoccupied with the causes of death and burdened by feelings of guilt (which tie him/her strongly to the past), it will be impossible for him/her to change his/her behavior patterns and emotional frames of reference. Guilt is the cornerstone of neurosis and a retarding factor in a child's normal emotional and social development. This is all the more true when the guilt is related to the trauma of the loss of a parent. The bereaved child can, therefore, be helped to go through the process of mourning and to readjust by being helped to understand the causes of death rationally and by being given emotional support.

D. The Concept of Inevitability of Death and its Effect on Mourning and Readjustment of Children

The concept of Inevitability involves regarding death as a natural phenomenon which is inevitable by the nature of things. Understanding the inevitability of death means perceiving death as a *universal* phenomenon, which applies to all living beings. Correct conceptualization of death's inevitability is important in the last stage of mourning, the state of reorganization. Moreover, it indirectly affects perception of death's causality. When the child understands that death is universal and that a person must eventually die of one cause or another, he/she will more readily understand the real causes of death. Moreover, such perception will diminish feelings of guilt, since it will help the child to understand that death, being a universal phenomenon, is not likely to have been caused by his/her anger, for instance. Perception of death as inevitable can ease the pain of the bereaved child: The bereaved child feels isolated and different, set apart from other children by his/her tragedy and loss. The realization that every child's parents must eventually die, may help the child to accept the inevitable, at the end of the mourning process, and to find a measure of comfort in the fact that death must come to all.

E. The Concept of Old Age — Rationale for its Inclusion in Questionnaire

The four concepts discussed above reflect the connection between cognitive perception and the emotional processes of mourning and readjustment of children. We have included an additional concept in the questionnaire: Old Age. This concept is related to conceptualization of death but is not related to mourning. Perception of Old Age means understanding the biological sequence of life, which consists of birth, growth, aging, and death. The concept of Old Age is related to the concepts of Causality and Inevitability, but we found, on the basis of a pilot study, that it was necessary to include specific questions on Old Age in order to examine a child's conceptualization of death. We found that a child may understand the concepts of Causality and Inevitability in connection with death but not as they related to old age. A child may say that old age is a cause of death and fail to understand that all people age; conversely, he/she may understand that everyone must age and fail to understand that everyone must die. When examining a bereaved child by means of the questionnaire, we also consider the *total score for conceptualization of death*, which includes the concept of Old Age, or we may take into account, differentially, only the four concepts which are related to the process of mourning and readjustment. The first four concepts are particularly significant for purposes of diagnosis and intervention. For purposes of research and for a complete picture of a child's (or group of children's) conceptualization of death, the concept of Old Age and the total score on conceptualization of death, which includes this concept, should be referred to.

F. Conceptualization of Animal Death

In addition to the questions relating to human death, we have composed a parallel series of identical questions (changing only the subjects, i.e., dog in place of person) relating to animal death. This parallelism between the questions relating to humans and the questions relating to animals contributed to research reliability and to consistency in scoring. Moreover, it leads to a better understanding of a child's conceptualization of death. Death is a phenomenon which applies to all living things, and to gain understanding of a child's conceptualization of death, we must discover how the child perceives human death as well as animal death. In addition, the parallelism of the questions provides us with further indicators for purposes of diagnosis and intervention. If, for instance, a child is able to conceptualize animal death but is unable to conceptualize parallel concepts related to human death, we may conclude that the child has emotional problems which prevent normal conceptualization of human death, and then help the child accordingly.

3. **Diagnostic Summary Record of an Individual Child's Conceptualization of Death**

Sara Smilansky

Child's Name_____Age_____Sex_____

Examiner's Name_____Date_____

A. Child's Scores on Human Death

CONCEPTS	Possible Score	Child's Score
1. Non-Reversibility	0 - 3	
2. Finality	0 - 3	
3. Causality	0 - 3	
4. Inevitability	0 - 3	
5. Old Age	0 - 3	
6. Total Score for Human Death	0 - 15	

B. Child's Scores on Animal Death

CONCEPTS	Possible Score	Child's Score
1. Non-Reversibility	0 - 3	
2. Finality	0 - 3	
3. Causality	0 - 3	
4. Inevitability	0 - 3	
5. Old Age	0 - 3	
6. Total Score for Animal Death	0 - 15	

203

C. Child's Scores on Conceptualization of Death

CONCEPTS		Possible Score	Child's Score
1.	Total Score for Human Death	0 - 15	
2.	Total Score for Animal Death	0 - 15	
3.	Total Conceptualization of Death	0 - 30	

D. Child's Scores on Four Factors of Death (based on factor analysis)

FACTORS		Possible Score	Child's Score
1.	*Non-Reversibility* Concept on Human plus Non-reversibility on Animal Death	0 - 6	
2.	*Finality* Concept on Human plus Finality on Animal Death	0 - 6	
3.	*Causality* Concept on Human plus Causality on Animal Death	0 - 6	
4.	*Inevitability* Concept on Human plus Inevitability on Animal Death plus Old Age on Human plus Old Age on Animal Death	0 - 12	
5.	Total Conceptualization of Death	0 - 30	

4. Psychometric Characteristics of the Questionnaire
(1. Sample 2. Construction of instrument 3. Validity 4. Reliability)

1. Sample: Construction of the questionnaire is based on a sample of 1,242 children, ranging in age from pre-kindergarten to, and including, fifth grade. Some are from poorly educated families while others are from well educated families. The sample includes 474 orphans* and 768 non-orphans (control). The orphan-population includes children orphaned in various ways: Army casualties, work-related accident casualties, road-accident casualties, deaths following illness, and others. The 768 non-orphans served as the control group for the orphans and they represent the child-population studying in the same classes as the orphans and coming from the same socio-economic background.

Choice of Sample: The sample population was chosen from kindergarten and elementary schools in four large cities in different parts of Israel. The sample includes all the orphans in the kindergartens and schools in the sample. From each class where there was an orphan, two non-orphans were chosen, identical with the orphan in sex, age, country of origin of the parents and level of parent's education. In certain cases only one child in the orphan's class served in the control group (if a second child of similar background could not be found); this did not, however, affect the control group as a whole. There was a large control group for each age group.

2. Construction of the Instrument − the Questionnaire: The Questionnaire is composed of two parts: Questions relating to human death and questions relating to animal death. Four psychologists served as judges to help in evaluating and selecting the questions, following two pilot studies. The questions chosen were those to which we got clear answers from the children and which, in our opinion and that of the judges were relevant to one of the five concepts composing the conceptualization of death: Irreversibility, Finality, Causality, Inevitability, and Old Age. We found that for

---

*   The word orphan in this book refers to a child that lost one parent (father or mother) through death.

certain concepts, such as Old Age, one question for humans and one for animals was sufficient for obtaining an answer which covers the concept. For other concepts, such as Finality, we found it necessary to include several questions in order to obtain a reliable picture of the child's understanding of the concept.

The scoring was based on our wish to maintain a clear structural division among the five concepts, so that the child's answers to the specific questions on each concept determine the score for that concept.

Equal weight was given to each of the five concept areas composing the conceptualization of death. The possible score for each concept is 0-3 points. Scoring rationale and maximum score are the same for each concept (see instructions for scoring). The total of the scores for the five concepts of death as related to humans constitutes the score for conceptualization of human death. The possible total score is 0-15 points. The total of the scores for the five concepts of death as related to animals, constitutes the score for conceptualization of animal death. The possible total scores is 0-15 points. The general score for conceptualization of death is arrived at, by addition of the score on animal death to the score on human death — a possible score of 0-30 points.

3. Validity

a) Construct Validity determines to what extent the questionnaire examines one significant characteristic and what factors contribute to the total score of the examinee being examined by the questionnaire.

We examined the following assumptions:

1. That all the questions in the Questionnaire for Examination of Human and Animal Death Conceptualization do indeed examine one central factor — i.e. conceptualization of death.

2. That there is empirical justification for the theoretical division of the conceptualization of death into five different concepts.

Construct calidity was examined by means of the technique and principal components of factor analysis. The results of the analysis through the method of principal components indicate that the Questionnaire examines one general characteristic — conceptualization of death.

206

This Questionnaire, similarly to an intelligence test, can be scored not only on the basis of one general factor but also on the basis of several factors, each of which examines a specific aspect of conceptualization of death. See page 212 How to score.

From among the various possible solutions suggested by the factor analysis, we decided upon four factors as specific indices. This solution seemed the best suited to our approach and was the closest to a simple structure (a desirable solution in factor analysis is one in which each factor is loaded only with items related to it and each item loads one factor only). This solution of four factors explains approximately 67 % of the total variation.

The following is the factor design resulting from factor analysis by four factors.

Childrens scores based on their answers to the 26 questions*	FACTORS			
	I. Irreversibility in Human and Animal Death	II. Finality in Human and Animal Death	III. Causality in Human and Animal Death	IV. Inevitability* of Human and Animal Death
1. Irreversibility of Human Death	.56	.13	.01	-.00
2. Irreversibility of Animal Death	.87	-.10	-.00	.02
3. Finality of Human Death	.07	.85	-.00	.03
4. Finality of Animal Death	.18	.53	.06	.03
5. Causality of Human Death	.05	.05	.49	.04
6. Causality of Animal Death	-.04	-.02	.66	-.02
7. Inevitability of Human Death	.03	.08	-.03	.71
8. Old Age in Human Death	.03	.08	-.05	.53
9. Inevitability of Animal Death	.04	-.11	.01	.81
10. Old Age in Animal Death	.01	.01	.14	.50

*including Old-Age

The factor analysis was based on the answers of the 768 non-orphans. The question which was now posed was whether the factors design obtained from the sample of orphans would be similar to that of the controls (non-orphans). A parallel factor analysis was carried out for the sample of 474 orphans, and the results for this group showed an almost absolute correlation to that of the normative group (the control group of non-orphans). The degree of similarity between the factors of the two groups was examined by means of the technique of factor matching.

Following are the coefficients of congruence of the four factors for the two samples (orphans and control (non-orphans):

Factors	I	II	III	IV
Coefficients of congruence	.962	.960	.860	.963

The results of the factor analysis provide an empirical basis for our theoretical assumptions regarding the division of the death conceptualization into concepts. In addition, they confirm our scoring system.

b) Criterion Related Validity examines the correlation between what is being examined by the questionnaire and other relevant indices, which are external criteria. Such validity would indicate that the questionnaire can be used to predict specific behavior which is theoretically related to the characteristic examined by the questionnaire.

The criterion related validity of he questionnaire was examined by means of the correlation between the children's scores for their answers to the 26 questions in the questionnaire and: 1) their I.Q. score; 2) their age.

1. Correlation between conceptualization of death and I.Q.

Since the questionnaire is meant to examine what a child knows about death and concepts related to death, a positive correlation may be expected to exist between the children's knowledge and concepts in the area being examined by the questionnaire and their general knowledge and concepts (unrelated to death) examined by means of an intelligence test. Such correlation will serve as one of the indices of criterion related validity.

Correlation was calculated by correlating a child's score on the questionnaire and the sum of his/her scores on two subtests of the

Wechsler intelligence test for children: The subtest of "knowledge" plus the subtest of "comprehension."

We found a significant Pearson correlation of .43 (P .001). This correlation was calculated on the basis of the scores of 552 children ranging in age from four to eight. The scores of children above this age were excluded from this calculation because at this age the children's answers related to most areas of death usually reach a peak, while no "peak" exists in the intelligence subtests.

The positive correlation which was found indicates that there is a connection between a child's knowledge about and conceptualization of death and his/her knowledge about and conceptualization of general subjects (unrelated to death). There is, however, no congruence between the two areas of "knowledge" and "comprehension". The questionnaire examines areas of knowledge different from those examined by the intelligence test. General intelligence is, however, significantly correlated to conceptualization of death.

2. Correlation between conceptualization of death and age

One of the criteria for validity of an intelligence test is that the raw score rises with age. Since the questionnaire examined cognitive development, it may be expected that the score on the questionnaire should rise with age. In our case, the grade in which the child was, served as the index of age, and the Pearson correlation was calculated between the child's score on conceptualization of death and his grade.

The correlation was calculated based on the scores of 552 children ranging in age from four to eight. Children above this age group were excluded from the calculations because of the 'peaking phenomenon' mentioned .above. A correlation of .56 (.001) was found between children's scores on the questionnaire and their age.

4. Reliability

The reliability of the questionnaire was examined by means of two methods:

1. Test-retest reliability
2. Interitem consistency

a) Test-Retest Reliability

Out of the sample of 1,242 children, one out of ten was chosen at random. These 124 children were given a repeat examination by means of the questionnaire, approximately four weeks after they had been examined with the other children of the entire sample. The coefficient of correlation between the total scores of the 124 children on their first examination and the total scores of their repeat examination was .0.84. Since the children could not have remembered the exact answers they had given to 26 questions during their first examination, it may be considered that such a high coefficient of correlation indicates the effectiveness of the Questionnaire for Examination of Death Concepts for children aged four to twelve.

b) Interitem Consistency

Interitem consistency was examined with a sample of 768 children ranging in age from four to ten. Interitem consistency examined the extent to which the individual items in the examination contribute to the general score, i.e., the conceptual consistency of the examination. Reliability based on interitem consistency was examined by means of the Kronbach Alpha, which is based on the correlation between the individual items and the total conceptualization of death. A correlation of = 77 was found, with all items contributing positively (that is, the exclusion of any one item would reduce the value of Alpha). Since the questionnaire is scored separately for concepts relating to human death and those relating to animal death, we calculated separate indices for each.

5. Guide: Administration and Scoring of the "Questionnaire for Examination of Human and Animal Death Conceptualization of Children"

1 Description of Questionnaire

The Questionnaire for Examination of Death Concepts is composed of two parts. The first part (13 questions) examines conceptualization of human death, and the second part (13 questions) examines the conceptualization of animal death. The questions for humans and animals are identical, with the exception of some of the references (i.e., 'Of what do *people* die?' as opposed to 'Of what do *dogs* die?'). All questions directly examine the child's understanding of various aspects of death. The first question in each part is a 'warmup' question and is not included in the scoring.

2. *Guide: How to Administer and How to Score the "Questionnaire for Examination of Human and Animal Death Conceptualization of Children"*

A. Instructions to be followed in the course of the examination.

The child is to be examined individually, in the form of a personal interview. The interviewer will ask the questions and record the answers (exactly in the words the child says them) in the appropriate place in the questionnaire form. (See page 195)

It is recommended that the interviewer converse with the child for a few minutes before presenting the questions dealing with death. In this way a relaxed atmosphere will be established. The child may be asked such general questions as "What is your name?", "Where do you live?", etc.

The questions to the child should be simple and matter-of-fact and constitute a natural continuation of the opening conversation (it is important that the interviewer's tone of voice should also be matter-of-fact, without a tone of fear or sadness). The interviewer might say, "I'm going to ask you some questions so that I can learn what you think about all kinds of things. I'll write down what you say so that I won't forget it."

Following these instructions the interviewer will ask the first question in the questionnaire regarding death concepts related to humans and so continue one question after the other until question 26.

The transition between the first part of the questionnaire (questions related to the death of humans) and its second part (questions related to the death of animals) should be smooth and the child should not be made aware that a new subject is being introduced.

The child should not be prompted or told whether his/her answer is correct or not. The interviewer might respond in some noncommittal manner or, if the child asks if his answer is correct, the interviewer might say, "You're doing fine. Now let's finish all the questions first, and then we can discuss your answers."

From our experience in administering the questionnaire to hundreds of children, it can be noted that children will willingly cooperate with the interviewer although he/she is a perfect stranger. Children like showing what they know and enjoy being taken seriously. They enjoy the idea of the interviewer listening to them attentively and recording their answers.

Since the subject of death is a sensitive subject for adults, some may hesitate to bring it up in a conversation with children. Adults are often surprised at the natural and matter-of-fact response of children to questions about death.

B. Analysis of the Child's Answers

The questionnaire is a standardized examination with a defined system for scoring and interpretation: Analysis of the answers must take into consideration two aspects:

1. The child's quantitative scores
2. The quality of the child's answers and his/her explanations.

A combined view of the quantitative and qualitative indices will make possible a reliable diagnosis of the child's conceptualization of death, and will be helpful in locating problematic areas in the child's conceptualization of death.

C. Quantitative Evaluation: Scoring

The questionnaire enables to obtain several possible scores:

1. A score for each of the five concepts, which comprise the concept of human death.

Based on the child's answers a separate score is given for each of the five concepts contained in the concept of human death: Non-reversibility; Finality; Causality; Inevitability; Old Age (see "Diagnostic Record of an Individual Child's Conceptualization of Death," page 203). The scale of scores for each concept is 0-3 and is based on a score key which will be introduced later.

2. A total score for conceptualization of human death.

The total score is a sum total of the scores on the five concepts of human death (See "Diagnostic Record," page 203). The sum total score can be 0-15.

3. A score for each of the five concepts which comprise the concept of animal death (See "Diagnostic Record", page 203).

Based on the child's answers, a separate score is given for each of the five concepts contained in the concept of animal death (in the same manner as is done for human death): Non-Reversibility; Finality; Causality; Inevitabilitu; Old Age.

4. A total score for conceptualization of animal death.

The total score of animal death is a sum total of the scores on the five concepts of animal death (see "Diagnostic Record", page 203). The sum total score can be 0-15.

5. Inclusive Score on Conceptualization of Death.

The sum of the five scores on conceptualization of *human death* *plus* the five scores on conceptualization of *animal death*, produces the inclusive score of Death Conceptualization (see "Diagnostic Record", page 204). The inclusive score can be 0-30.

6. A score for each of the four factors, based on the results of the factor analysis.

By means of factor-analysis, we arrived at four factors which parallel the five concepts of human death and the five concepts of animal death (See "Diagnostic Record", page 204).

Factor 1 is the sum of the child's scores on Non-reversibility in human death plus in animal death. The scale of scores is 0-6

Factor 2 is the sum of the child's scores on Finality in human death plus in animal death. The scale of scores is 0-6.

Factor 3 is the sum of the child's scores on Causality in human death plus in animal death. The scale of scores is 0-6.

Factor 4 is the sum of the child's scores on Inevitability in human death plus Inevitability in animal death, plus Old-age in human death plus Old-age in animal death. The scale of scores is 0-12 (See "Diagnostic Record, page 204). *Method of Scoring and Recording and Scoring Key:*

213

A. Scoring the five concepts for human death and for animal death.

It must be emphasized that only the scores on the five concepts of human death and the five concepts of animal death are directly based on the child's answers to the 26 questions in the questionnaire. The scores for the four factors are based on the scores of the ten concepts (See "Diagnostic Record", page 204).

The answers given by the child and their exact wording and explanations are important during the stage of quantitative and qualitative analysis.

The scoring of the five concepts for human death and the five concepts of animal death respectively, follows a detailed key, to be introduced later. For each concept, the score is determined and based on the child's answers, as evaluated according to the scoring key.

The child's scores should be recorded in the appropriate columns in the "Diagnostic Record of an Individual Child's Conceptualization of Death" (See pages 203 and 204).

B. Scoring key for the concept of irreversibility in human death.

The score is determined on the basis of the child's answers to questions 7 and 8.

Question 7: "If a person dies and has been in his grave for some time, can he return to become a living person?" "Why?"

Question 8: "If a person dies and has not yet been buried, can he return to become a living person?" "Why?"

A score of 3 will be given if the child has given correct answers to both questions and suitable explanations for both answers.

Sample for satisfactory answer: "No, a dead person will not be a real person again because he's dead and he won't be alive again." Sufficient justification would be answers such as, "Because he's dead," "Because he can't", or "Because he was old and he died."

A score of 2 is given for two correct answers and one correct explanation. The score of 2 can be given in two cases:
- If the child has answered both questions correctly but has given an explanation only to one question.
- If the child has answered both questions correctly and has given an explanation to each question but only *one* of his two explanations is correct.

Examples of unsatisfactory justification: "Because the soldiers don't want him to live;" "Because the doctors don't want him to be alive again," or "Because he was injured."

A *score of 1* will be given if the child has answered one question correctly, with one correct explanation. Children will generally answer that a person who has been buried cannot return to become a living person but if he has not been buried, he can. A score of one is also given if the child answers both answers correctly but his justifications of both answers are wrong.

A *score of 0* is given if the child has answered both questions incorrectly, or has failed to answer, or has answered one question correctly but its explanation is incorrect.

Summary Table for Scoring the Concept of Irreversibility in Human Death

Score	No. of Correct Answers		No. of Correct Explanations
3	2	plus	2
2	2	plus	1
1	1	plus	1
	2	plus	0
0	1	plus	0
	0	plus	0

C. *Scoring key for the concept of Finality in human death.*

The scoring is determined on the basis of the following five questions in the questionnaire:

Question No. 5. "Does a dead person know that he is dead? Why?"

Question No. 6. "Is a dead person able to feel? Does he feel pain? Why?"

Question No. 9. "Can a dead person see? Why?"

Question No. 10. "Can a dead person hear? Why?"

Question No. 11. "Can a dead person move? Why?"

A *score of 3* is given if all the five answers and their explanations are correct. The child will get a score of 3 for negative answers ("No") to all five questions and for good explanations to the five answers. A correct explanation, for instance for question No. 11 would be "Because he's dead." An incorrect explanation would be "Because there is a lot of soil and a large stone on top of him." A false answer of this nature shows a lack of understanding of the concept of Finality as related to mobility. Thus, despite the correct answers, the child will not earn a score of 3.

A score of 2 will be given if the answer to only *one* of the five questions is wrong or if one of the five explanations shows lack of understanding.

The child will receive a score of 2 for the following answers and explanations:

1. Answering only one question of the five incorrectly.
2. Giving an incorrect explanation (justification) for one of his answers, though all five answers may be correct.

For instance, if the child has answered to question No. 9 that a dead person cannot see, but justified it incorrectly by saying "Because the grave is dark." To sum up positively, a score of 2 is given for four correct answers with four correct explanations; and for five correct answers with only four correct explanations and justifications. As a general rule, a wrong explanation (justification) will disqualify a correct answer.

A score of 1 will be given when two of the answers to the five questions are incorrect or if two explanations (although the answers may be correct) show a lack of understanding. To state it positively, a child will earn a score of 1 for correctly answering and correctly explaining three out of the five questions.

A score of 0 (zero) will be given to a child who has answered correctly three questions but explained correctly only two; or a child who has answered only two questions correctly with two correct justifications; or has answered fewer questions or none at all.

Summary Table for Scoring the Concept of Finality in Human Death

Score	No. of Correct Answers		No. of Correct Explanations
3	5	plus	5
2	5	plus	4
	4	plus	4
1	4	plus	3
	3	plus	3
0	3	plus	2
	2	plus	2
	1	plus	1
	0	plus	0

D. Scoring Key for the Concept of Causality in Human Death

The score is determined on the basis of the child's a answers to question 2 — ."Of what do people die? Of what other reasons can people die?"

A score of 3 is given for an answer citing old age and at least one other correct cause of death, such as a war or an accident, etc.

A score of 2 is given if the child has cited only old age.

A score of 1 is given if the child has cited at least one correct cause of death but has failed to cite old age as a cause. Possible correct answers: 'Of illness,' 'Of shooting, bombing or poison," or "When they are sick.' Answers such as 'lightning' or 'arrows' are also considered correct. Answers such as 'Of a headache' or 'Because they are cursed by a witch' or 'Of roaches' are unacceptable.

A score of 0 (zero) is given when the child has answered incorrectly, failing to produce even one correct cause of death, or has not answered at all.

E. Scoring Key for the Concept of Inevitability in Human Death

The score is determined on the basis of the child's answers to question 13 — "Does everyone die?" "Why?" If the child has answered "no" and has not explained, he should be asked "Who does die?".

217

A score of 3 is given if the child, recognizing the universality of death's inevitability, has answered that all people, without exception, must die and will eventually die. The child's explanation of "Why" must also be acceptable. An answer such as "Because everyone gets old" would be correct.

A score of 2 is given if the child recognizes the principle of Inevitability but makes an individual exception. Three possible answers would get a score of 2:

1. If the child says that everyone must die but excludes himself.
2. If the child says that not everyone dies, but only old people, and that he/she will die only when he/she is old.
3. If the child has answered that everyone must eventually die but failed to explain this answer correctly.

A score of 1 is given if the child considers death's inevitability limited and related to one specific cause or to one specific group of people. The following answers would rate a score of 1:

1. If the child considers death's inevitability related to causes other than old age and answers, for instance, "No, not everyone dies, but only those who are sick."
2. If the child answers "No, not everyone, only the very, very old."
3. If the child excludes other people, in addition to himself, from death's inevitability and gives an answer such as "Only I and my father and mother won't die" or "only mean people die."

A score of 0 (zero) will be given if the child has not answered at all or given an answer such as "Nobody has to die."

F. *Scoring Key for the Concept of Old Age in Human Death*

The score is determined on the basis of the answers to question 3 — "Who gets old? Does everyone get old?." If the child answers "No," ask "Who does get old?".

A score of 3 is given if the child understands that everyone ages and that he himself/she herself will get old. Children sometimes qualify their answers. If the child's answer contains one of the following two qualifications, it is till considered correct:

1. Not everyone gets old because some people die before they get old.
2. The child says that he/she will get old but after a long, long

time, or that he/she will be old only when he/she is a grand-father/grandmother.

A score of 2 is given if the child says that everyone gets old but cites a specific person or group of persons as an exception, as in one of the following answers:

1. If the child says that he/she will get old but not all others will.
2. If the child says that all people get old but that he/she will not.
3. If the child says that only some people get old, like grand-father, and that the child himself/herself will also get old, but other people will not.

A score of 1 is given if the child says that a large part of all human beings will get old, as in the following answers:

1. If the child answers that a specific person will get old but that he/she will not. For instance, "My uncle will get old, but I won't."
2. If the child does not mention someone else who will get old but says that he/she will.
3. If he answers correctly, but his explanation shows faulty understanding.

A score of 0 (zero) is given if the child fails to answer or answers that nobody (including himself) will ever get old.

G. Scoring Key for the Five Concepts of Animal Death

Scoring for conceptualization of animal death follows the same principles and guidelines applied in the scoring of conceptualization of human death. Each of the five concepts for animal death has a possible score of 0-3 and the scoring key is identical to that used in human death. Obviously, the wording of the questions is slightly different, and the questions on animal death will substitute words such as 'dog' or 'cat' for words such as 'person' or in questions on human death. There are several minor differences between the scoring of human death and the scoring of animal death, as follows:

The Concept of Inevitability — A child's score for animal death will not decline as significantly is he/she excludes his/her pet from the inevitability of death, as it will decline for human death if he/she excludes himself/herself from death. For Inevitability in animal death the score will be lowered from 3 to 2 points if the child ex-cludes his pet from the animals that must die.

The Concept of Old Age — As in the scoring of human death, the score in animal death will decline if the child excludes his/her pet from the animals that get old.

A score of 3 will be given for an answer such as "Yes, I think that all dogs will get old."

A score of 2 will be given for an answer such as "All dogs get old but my dog won't."

A score of 1 will be given for an answer such as "Not all animals get old; some do and some don't. Horses never get old."

Scoring and Recording in the "Diagnostic Record of an Individual Child's Conceptualization of Death" (See page 203 and 204).

To obtain the total score for human death, add the scores of the five concepts of human death. Similarly, to obtain the total score for animal death, add the scores of the five concepts of animal death (the possible total score in each category is 0-15). Enter the total score for each category in the appropriate column in the "Diagnostic Record" (See page 203).

To obtain the total score for conceptualization of death add the total score for human death to the total score for animal death. The possible score is 0-30. Enter the total score for conceptualization of death in the appropriate column in the "Diagnostic Record" (See page 204).

H. Scoring Key and Recordings for the Four Factors

Factor 1 — Non-reversibility in Human and Animal Death

To obtain the child's score for Factor 1, add his/her scores on Non-reversibility of human death (Diagnostic Record Table A — Concept 1) plus Non-reversibility of animal death (Diagnostic Record Table B — Concept 1). Record the resulting score in the Diagnostic Record Table D — Factor 1.

Factor 2 — Finality in Human and Animal Death

To obtain the child's score for Factor 2, add his/her scores on Finality in human death (Diagnostic Record Table A — Concept 2) plus Finality in animal death (Diagnostic Record Table B — Concept 2). Enter the resulting score in Diagnostic Record Table D — Factor 2.

Factor 3 — Causality in Human and Animal Death

To obtain the child's score for Factor 3, add his/her scores on Causality in human death (Diagnostic Record Table A — Concept 3)

220

plus causality in animal death (Diagnostic Record Table B – Concept 3). Enter the resulting score in Diagnostic Record Table D – Factor 3.

Factor 4 – Inevitability and Old-Age in Human and Animal Death

To obtain the child's score for Factor 4, add his/her scores in Inevitability of human death (Diagnostic Record Table A – Concept 4) plus Old Age in human death (Diagnostic Record Table A – Concept 5) plus Inevitability in animal death (Diagnostic Record Table B – Concept 4) plus Old Age in animal death (Diagnostic Record Table B – Concept 5). Enter the sum total of the above four scores in the Diagnostic Record Table D – Factor 4.

6. Quantitative and Qualitative Diagnosis

Quantitative analysis is the first stage in diagnosing a child's conceptualization of death. (See "Diagnostic summary record of an individual child's conceptualization of death" pages: 203-204) It enables us to determine what level the child has reached in understanding the various concepts of death. Quantitative scores are, therefore, sufficient for purposes of research or diagnosis of a group of children, such as all the children in a class in school. For a better understanding of the individual child, however, in addition to the quantitative analysis, qualitative analysis is to be desired. The Questionnaire for Examination of Death Conceptualization can also serve in qualitative analysis.

Qualitative analysis involves studying the original verbal answers given by the child for the purpose of determining whether there are certain emotional difficulties related to specific concepts of death.

Our study showed that three concepts of death may serve to indicate a child's emotional problems related to death. These are: Causality, Non-reversibility, and Finality. Thus, when evaluating the individual child's conceptualization of death and attitude to death, one must, following the stage of quantitative analysis, return to the questionnaire for a closer look at the child's answers and explanations to the questions relating to Causality, Non-reversibility, and Finality in human death. We found that there are a number of indicators which may suggest that the child has specific problems. These indicators are as follows:

A. An incorrect answer which is qualitatively far below the general level of the other answers given by the child. The following case will serve as illustration.

An eight-year-old child who scored average or above on all other concepts of death, had a very low score on Causality in human death. A study of his answers revealed that the low score on Causality stemmed from an exceptionally poor answer to the question "Of what do people die? Of what other reasons can people die?" The child's answer was, "Of headache. Or when people make you angry." This was a surprisingly poor answer when compared to the child's other answers. Such an answer may suggest misinformation or an emotional problem. In this case, since the level of all the other answers excludes the possibility of a cognitive lack, it would be safe to assume that the child in question has certain emotional problems related to Causality of human death. The child's score on Causality in animal death was considerably higher than the score in human death. It must be remembered that the concept of Causality plays an important role in the process of mourning as well as readjustment to the new reality. This bereaved child tends to blame himself for the death of the loved one, and these feelings of guilt make it difficult for him in his mourning process and in his coping in new reality. Appropriate help given to the child mentioned above would help him first to gain a cognitive understanding of the Causality of death, and, subsequently, to be able to accept emotionally the real cause of death.

B. An emotionally 'saturated' answer, usually relating a story in which the child plays a part and often containing a dream or imaginary story. The relevant question is not whether the story is imaginary or not, but rather what the significance of the child's imaginary world is. The following case will serve as illustration:

A five-year-old boy whose father was deceased answered the question "Of what do people die? Of what other reasons can people die?" with this story: "Once a boy went to the army with his father. Some thieves came so the boy shot at them with his father's gun. The thieves didn't shoot back at me because they didn't see me, because I was little, real tiny. But then father went to the army so they shot at him and killed him.' It is clear from the child's answer that he considered himself to blame, to a certain extent, for his father's death. This child obviously needs help in solving the emotional problem with which he is burdened.

C. Failure to answer the question related to a certain concept of death. Following is a case in point:

A six-year-old boy whose answers to most of the questions show a high level of understanding gave the answer 'I don't know' to questions relating to non-reversibility in human death. His behavior while answering the question indicated an unwillingness to touch upon the subject. The same child gave correct answers to questions relating to Non-reversibility in animal death. This would suggest that the child was trying to evade a painful subject which he had difficulty in dealing with. This child, too, needs help in solving the emotional problem with which he is burdened.

D. Bizarre elements in the child's answers. The examiner usually has difficulty in following such an answer and making sense of it for purposes of recording it. The examiner may suddenly feel that the child is talking nonsense. The following example will serve to illustrate:

A five-year-old boy whose father has been killed in a car accident answered all the questions satisfactorily and the general level of his conceptualization of death was high. When it came to the question "Of what do people die?", however, he answered, "In a storm, from a falling brick, in the evening." This answer would merit a score of zero. It differed sharply from all the child's other answers and indicated an emotional problem.

A further example: An eight-year-old orphaned boy, a very intelligent child, answered all the questions nicely. When it came to the question "Can a dead person hear?", however, he answered, "Yes, he can hear his children. Some dead people have an antenna in their grave and this antenna is connected to an instrument with lots of dials, like a radio. When he is buried, the dials are adjusted so that he can always hear what is happening outside the grave."

E. A score on conceptualization of human death which is significantly lower than the score on animal death.

7. Possible uses of the Questionnaire

The questionnaire is a simple test, in both administration and scoring. Any adult, after reading the guide and a certain amount of experience in examining several children, should be able to use the questionnaire for purposes of determining a given child's level of conceptualization of death. Teachers, for instance, can use it on students in their class, and a sufficiently well-educated mother can use it on her child.

The child's answers show the level of his/her understanding of the various concepts related to death. Comparison of the child's score with the average score of his age group according to the appropriate norm table will show his/her relative level. The average of the scores of all the children in a kindergarten class will show the teacher the level of conceptualization of death of the children in her class.

Qualitative analysis of a child's answers makes possible more precise, differential diagnosis of the areas in conceptualization of death in which the child is having emotional difficulty.

The child's answers reveal the areas in which he/she lacks knowledge and/or her specific emotional difficulties. This diagnosis enables us to plan intervention and then use the questionnaire in order to assess change, as a result of the intervention.

Diagnosis of the child's level of conceptualizing death which is based on quantitative as well as qualitative analysis enables us to help the child, both on the cognitive and on the emotional level.

The Questionnaire for Examination of Death Concepts can be used not only as bases when we wish to help an individual child to gain a better conceptualization of death. It can serve to aid the teacher, counselor, or psychologists in planning a talk with children on the subject of death. Children often bring up the subject of death spontaneously. Occurrences such as finding a dead bird, the death of someone's grandfather, wars, and accidents raise many questions in children's minds. The questionnaire can be used by those working with children as a tool to begin and direct a discussion on the subject of death.

Part Seven:

BIBLIOGRAPHY

1, Alexander, I. et al. "Affectiveness Responses to Concept of Death in a Population of Children and Early Adolescents". In Fulton, R. *"Death and Identity"*, 1965.

2. Anthony, S. *"The Discovery of Death in Childhood and After"*. London: Allen Cane, 1971.

3. Astrachan, M. "Management of a Staff Death in a Children's Institution." *Child Welfare*, 1977, 56.

4. Barnes, M.J. "Reactions to the Death of a Mother". *The Psycho-analytic Study of the Child*, 1964, 19.

5. Bergmann, T. *"Children in the Hospital"*. N.Y. International University Press, 1965.

6. Black, D. "The Bereaved Child". *Journal of Child Psychology and Psychiatry and Allied Disciplines*, 1978, 19.

7. Brown, F. "Childhood Bereavement and Subsequent Psychiatric Disorders". *British Journal of Psychiatry*, 1966, 112.

8. Brown, G.I. *"The Live Classroom"*, N.Y. Viking, 1975.

9. Bryant, E.H. "Teacher in Crisis: a classmate is dying". *Elementary School Journal*, 1978, 78.

10. Cain, A. and Fast, I. "Children's Disturbed Reactions to the Death of a Sibling". *American Journal of Orthopsychiatry*, 1964, 34.

11. Cain, A. and Fast, I. "Children's Disturbed Reactions to Parent Suicide", *American Journal of Orthopsychiatry*, 1966, 36.

12. Cavenar, J.O., Nash, J.L. and Maltbie, A.A. "Anniversary Reactions Masquerading as Manic-Depressive Illness", *American Journal of Psychiatry*, 1977, 134.

227

13. Clay, V. "Children Deal with Death". *The School Counselor*, 1976, 23.

14. Deutch, M. and Brown, B. "Social influences in Negro-White Intelligence Affluence". *J. Social Issues*, 1964, 20 (2).

15. Delisle, R. and Woods, A. "Children and Death: Coping Models In Literature". *Psychotherapy: Theory, Research and Practice*, 1977, 14.

16. Deutsch, H. "A 2-year Old Boy's First Love Comes to Grief". In L. Jesser and E. Pavenstedt (Eds.) *"The Dynamic of Psychopathology in Childhood"*. N.Y. Grune & Stratton, 1959.

17. Elizur, E. and Kaffman, M. "Children's Reactions Following the Death of the Father: The First Four Years." *Journal of the American Academy of Child Psychiatry*, 1982, 21.

18. English, O. "The Psychological Role of the Father in the Family". *Social Case Work*, 1954, 35.

19. Evans, B.J. "The Death of a Classmate". *Journal of School Health*, 1982, 52.

20. Ewalt, P.L. and Perkins, L.L. "The Real Experience of Death Among Adolescents". *Social Casework*, 1979, 60.

21. Feifel, H. *"Meaning of Death"*. N.Y. McGraw Hill, Inc., 1959.

22. Feinberg, D. "Preventive Therapy with Siblings of a Dying Child". *Journal of the American Academy of Child Psychiatry*, 1970, 9.

23. Ferguson, F. "Children's Cognitive Discovery of Death". *Journal of the association for the Care of Children in Hospitals*, 1978, 7.

24. Fox, S.S. *"Good Grief: Helping Groups of Children When a Friend Dies"*. New England association for the Education of Young Children. Boston, M.A. 1985.

25. Fox, S.S. "Children's Anniversary Reactions to the Death of a Family Member". *Omega*, 1984-85, 15.

26. Freud, A. and Burlingham, D. *"War and Children"*. N.Y. International University Press, 1953.

27. Freud, S. "Mourning and Melancholia". In *Collected Papers*. N.Y. Basic Books, 1959.

28. Fulton, R. (Ed.) *"Death and Identity"*. N.Y. Wiley and Sons, 1965.

29. Furman, R. "Death of a six-year-old's mother during his analysis". *The Psychoanalytic Study of the Child*, 1964, 19.

30. Furman, R. "Death of the Young Child". *The Psychoanalytic Study of the Child*, 1964, 19.

31. Furmann R. "The Child's Reaction to Death in his Family". In B. Schoenberg (Ed.) *"Loss and Grief"*. N.Y. Columbia University Press, 1970.

32. Furman, R.A. "A Child's Capacity for Mourning". In *"The Child in His Family: The Impact of Disease and Death"*. E.J. Anthony and C. Koupernik (Eds). Wiley N.Y. 1973.

33. Furman, E. *"A Child's Parent Dies"*. New Haven: Yale University Press, 1974.

34. Furman, E. "Helping Children Cope with Death". *Young Children*, 1978, 33.

35. Gorer, G. *"Death, Grief and Mourning"*. Garden City N.Y., Doubleday and Company, 1965.

36. Grollman, E.A. *"Explaining Death to Children"*. Boston: Beacon Press, 1967.

37. Grollman, E. *"Talking About Death"*. Boston: Beacon Press, 1970.

38. Harper, B.C. *"Death: The Coping Mechanism of the Health Professional"*. Greenville, SC: Southeastern University Press, 1977.

39. Harris, W.H. "Some Reflections Concerning Approaches to Death Education". *Journal of School Health*, 1978, 48.

40. Henney, M. and Barnhart, R.S. "Death Education: Do We Need it?" *Psychological Reports*, 1980, 43.

41. Hilgard, J. et al. "Strength of Adult Ego Following Death and Childhood Bereavement". In Fulton, R. *"Death and Identity"*, 1965.

42. Hilgard, J. "Depressive and Psychotic States on Anniversaries of Sibling Death in Childhood". *International Psychiatry Clinics*, 1969, 6.

43. Hinton, J. *"Dying"*. Middlesex, Penguin Books, 1967.

44. Isaacs, S. *"Childhood and After"*. Routledge and Kegan, 1950.

45. Kastenbaum, R. and Aisenberg, R. *"The Psychology of Death"*. Spinger Publishing Co., 1972.

46. Kastenbaum, R.J. *"Death, Society and Human Experience."* Mosley, St. Louis, M.O. 1977.

47. Keith, C. and Ellis, D. "Reactions of Pupils and Teachers to Death in the Classroom". *The School Counselor*, 1978, 25.

48. Kliman, A.S. *"Crisis: Psychological First Aid for Recovery and Growth."* Holt, Rinehard and Winston, N.Y. 1978.

49. Kliman, G.W. *"Psychological Emergencies of Childhood"* Grune and Stratton, N.Y. 1968.

50. Kvell, R. and Rabkin, L. "The Effects of Sibling Death on the Surviving child: A Family Perspective. *Family Process*, 1979, 18.

51. Krementy, J. *"How it Feels When a parent Dies"*. Knopf, N.Y. 1983.

52. Kubler-Ross, E. *"On Death and Dying"*. McMillan Co., 1969.

53. Levinson, E. et.al. "Death Comes on an Eight Grader". In *"What Helped Me When my Loved one Died"*. Grollman E.A. (ed.) Beacon, Boston M.A. 1981.

54. Leviton, D. "Death Education". In Feifel, H. (Ed.) *"New Meanings of Death"*. McGraw Hill Book Co., 1977.

55. Lindsay, M. and McCarthy, D. "Caring for Brothers and Sisters of a Dying Child". In L. Burton (Ed.) *"Care of the Child Facing Death"*. Routledge and Kegan, 1974.

56. Lonetto, R. *"Children's Conceptions of Death"*. Springer, N.Y. 1980.

57. Kopez, T. and Kliman, G.W. "Memory, Reconstruction and Mourning in the analysis of a 4-Year-Old: Maternal Bereavement in the Second Year of Life". *Psychoanalytic Study of the Child*, 1979, 34.

58. McDonald, M. "Helping Children to Understand Death: An Experience with Death in a Nursery School". *Journal of Nursery Education*, 1963, 19.

59. Meathenia, P.S. "An Experience With Fear in the Lives of Children". *Childhood Education*, 1971, 48.

60. Miller, J.B. "Children's Reactions to the Death of a Parent: a Review of the Psychoanalytic Literature". *Journal of the American Psychoanalytic Assocation*, 1971, 19.

61. Mills, G. et al. *"Discussing Death"*. Homewood, Ill., ETC Pub., 1976.

62. Mitchell, N. *"The Child's Attitude to Death"*. N.Y., 1969.

63. Moriatry, P.M. (Ed.) *"The Loss of Loved Ones"*. Springfield, Ill., Charles C. Thomas, 1976.

64. Nagara, H. „Children's Reactions to the Death of Important Objects: A Developmental Approach". *Psychoanalytic Study of the Child*, 1966, 25.

65. Nagy, M. "The Child's View of Death". In Feifel, H. (Ed.) *"The Meaning of Death"*, McGraw-Hill, 1959.

66. Nelson, C. "Challenging the Last Great Taboo: Death". *The School Counselor*, 1975, 22.

67. Parness, E. "Effects of Experiences With Loss and Death Among Preschool Children". *Children Today*, 1975, 4 (G).

68. Piaget, J. *"The Child's Construction of Reality"*. Basic Books, 1955.

69. Pruett, K. "Home Treatment for Two Infants Who Witnessed their Mother's Murder". *Journal of the American Academy of Child Psychiatry*, 1979, 18.

70. Redl, F. and Wineman, D. *"Children Who Hate"*. N.Y. McMillan Co., 1951.

71. Rochlin, G. "How Young Children View Death and Themselves". In E. Grollman (Ed.) *"Talking about Death"*, Beacon Press, 1967.

72. Rosenthal, N.R. "Teaching Educators to Deal with Death". *Death Education*, 1978, 2 (G).

73. Rosenthal, P. and Rosenthal, S. "Suicidal Behavior by Preschool Children." *American Journal of Psychiatry*, 1984, 14.

74. Rudolph, M. *"Should the Children Know? Encounters with Death in the Lives of Children."* Schacken, N.Y. 1978.

75. Salady, S.A. and Royal, M.E. "Children and Death: Guidelines for Grief Work". *Child Psychiatry and Human Development*, 1981, 11.

76. Schlesinger, B. *"The One Parent Family"*. University of Toronto Press, 1970.

77. Sears, P.S. "Doll-play aggression in normal and young children, influence of sex, age, sibling status, father's absence". *Psychological Monographs: General and Applied*, 1951, 65, (6) IV, 42.

78. Sharapan, H. "Mister Rogers Neighborhood: Dealing with Death on a Children's Television Series." *Death Education*, 1977, 1.

79. Simos, B.G. *"A Time to Grieve: Loss as a Universal Human Experience"*. Family Service Association of America, N.Y. 1979.

80. Smilansky, S. "Learning, Social and Emotional Adjustment in Elementary School Orphans". In Spielberger, C.D., Sarason, I. G. and Milgram, N. (Eds.) *"Stress and Anxiety"*, Vol. 8, Hemisphere Pub. Co., 1981.

81. Smilansky, S. "Different Mourning Patterns and the Orphan's Intellectual Ability to Understand the Concept of Death". *Advances in Thanatology*, Vol. 5, No. 2, N.Y. Arno Press, 1981.

82. Smilansky, S. "Rehabilitation Worker's Confrontation with the

Needs of Israel Defence Forces' Orphans". In *Psychosocial Research in Rehabilitation"*. E. Lahav (edit.) Ministry of Defence Publishing House, 1982.

83. Smilansky, S. "The Parent as partner in the Educational Advancement of Preschool Age Children". In *"Early Childhood Education — An International Perspective"*. (edit.), N. Yaniv, B. Spodek and D. Steg. Plenum Press, N.Y. 1982.

84. Smilansky, S. "The Effect of Certain Learning Conditions on the Progress of Disadvantaged Children of Kindergarten Age." *Journal of School Psychology*, 1976, 4.

85. Smilansky, S. "Educational Programming for Young Children Across Cultures". In *"Current Issues in Child Development"*. (edit.) M. Scott and S. Grimmett, National Association for the Education of Young Children, Washington D.C. 1977.

86. *"Suggestions for Teachers and School Counselors"*. Oak Brook, Il. the Compassionate Friends, Inc. 1983.

87. Terr, L. "Children of Chowchilla: A Study of Psychic Trauma". *Psychoanalytic Study of the Child*, 1979, 34.

88. Terr, L. "Forbidden Games: Post-Traumatic Child's Play." *Journal of the American Academy of Child Psychiatry*, 1981, 20.

89. Terr, L. "Psychic Trauma in Children: Observations Following the Chowchilla School-bus Kidnapping". *American Journal of Psychiatry*, 1981, 138.

90. Terr, L. "Chowchilla Revisited: The Effects of Psychic Trauma Four Years After a School-bus Kidnapping". *American Journal of Psychiatry*, 1983, 140.

91. Tonbee, A. *"Man's Concern with Death"*. McGraw-Hill, 1969.

92. Watt, N.F. and Nicholi, A. "Early Death of a Parent as an Ethological Factor in Schizophrenia". *American Journal of Orthopsychiatry*, 1979, 49.

93. Weiss, H. and Shaak, Y. *"Helping Children with Death"*. McGraw-Hill, 1969.

94. Weisman, A. "Coping With Untinely Death." *Psychiatry*, 1973, 36.

95. Wolfenstein, M. "How is Mourning Possible". *The Psychoanalytic Study of the Child*, 1966, 21.

96. Wolfenstein, M. and Kliman, G. *"Children and the Death of a President"*. Doubleday Anchor, Garden City N.Y. 1966.

97. Worden, J.W. *"Grief Counseling and Grief Therapy: A Handbook for the Mental Health Practitioner"*. Springer, N.Y. 1982.

98. Yudkin, S. "Children and Death". *Lancet* 1967, 1.

Part Eight:

GRAPHS, TABLES AND SHORT DESCRIPTIONS OF STUDIES

Graph No 1   CONCEPTUALIZATION OF DEATH
              ACCORDING TO AGE (GRADES IN SCHOOL) & PARENTS EDUCATION

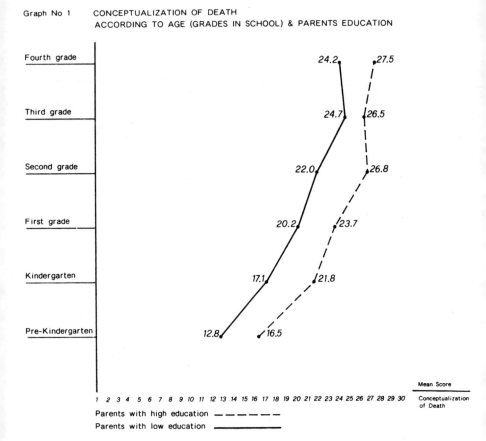

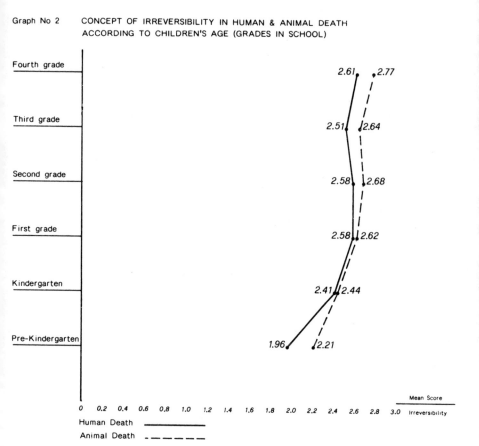

Graph No 2   CONCEPT OF IRREVERSIBILITY IN HUMAN & ANIMAL DEATH
ACCORDING TO CHILDREN'S AGE (GRADES IN SCHOOL)

Fourth grade   2.61 •2.77

Third grade   2.51 2.64

Second grade   2.58 2.68

First grade   2.58 2.62

Kindergarten   2.41 2.44

Pre-Kindergarten   1.96 2.21

```
                                                          Mean Score
0   0.2  0.4  0.6  0.8  1.0  1.2  1.4  1.6  1.8  2.0  2.2  2.4  2.6  2.8  3.0  Irreversibility
    Human Death  _____
    Animal Death  _ _ _ _ _ _
```

237

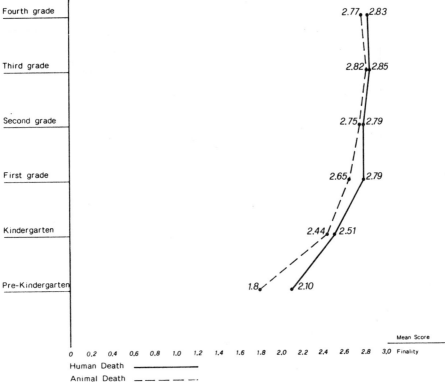

Graph No 3   CONCEPT OF FINALITY IN HUMAN & ANIMAL DEATH
              ACCORDING TO CHILDREN'S AGE (GRADES IN SCHOOL)

Fourth grade   2.77 2.83

Third grade   2.82 2.85

Second grade   2.75 2.79

First grade   2.65 2.79

Kindergarten   2.44 2.51

Pre-Kindergarten   1.8 2.10

                                                              Mean Score

0   0.2   0.4   0.6   0.8   1.0   1.2   1.4   1.6   1.8   2.0   2.2   2.4   2.6   2.8   3.0   Finality
Human Death _____
Animal Death _ __ __ __ __ _.

238

Graph No 4   CONCEPT OF CAUSALITY IN HUMAN & ANIMAL DEATH
              ACCORDING TO CHILDREN'S AGE (GRADES IN SCHOOL)

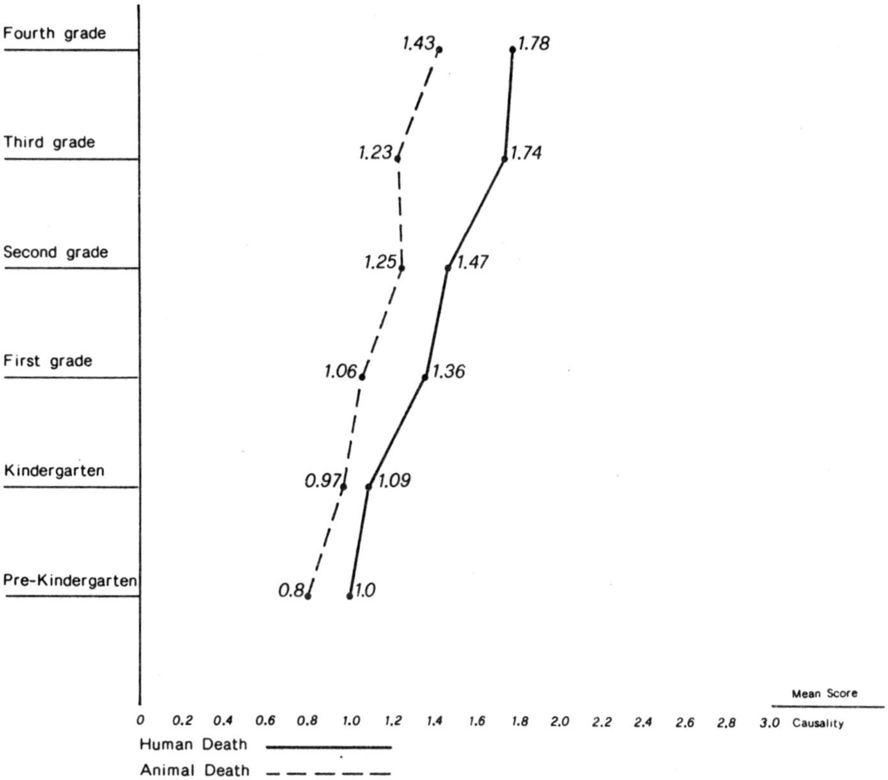

Fourth grade   1.43   1.78

Third grade   1.23   1.74

Second grade   1.25   1.47

First grade   1.06   1.36

Kindergarten   0.97 1.09

Pre-Kindergarten   0.8   1.0

Mean Score

0   0.2 0.4 0.6 0.8 1.0 1.2 1.4 1.6 1.8 2.0 2.2 2.4 2.6 2.8 3.0 Causality

Human Death ——————————
Animal Death — — — — — —

239

Graph No 5   CONCEPT OF INEVITABILITY IN HUMAN & ANIMAL DEATH
ACCORDING TO CHILDREN'S AGE (GRADES IN SCHOOL)

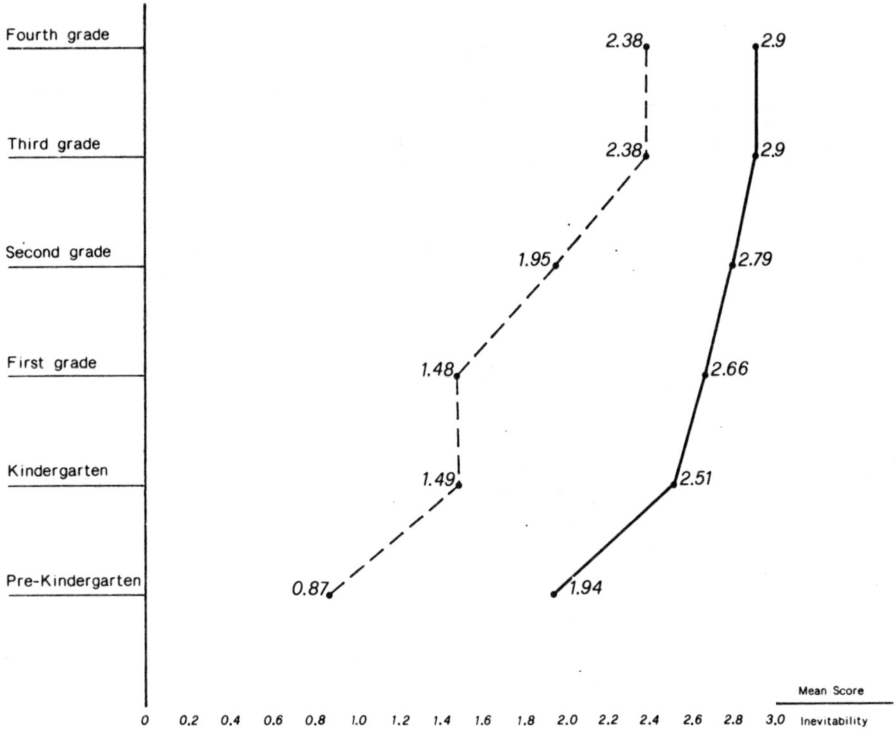

Fourth grade — 2.38 • / 2.9

Third grade — 2.38 • / 2.9

Second grade — 1.95 / 2.79

First grade — 1.48 / 2.66

Kindergarten — 1.49 / 2.51

Pre-Kindergarten — 0.87 / 1.94

Mean Score

0   0.2   0.4   0.6   0.8   1.0   1.2   1.4   1.6   1.8   2.0   2.2   2.4   2.6   2.8   3.0   Inevitability

Human Death   ————————————
Animal Death   — — — — — — .

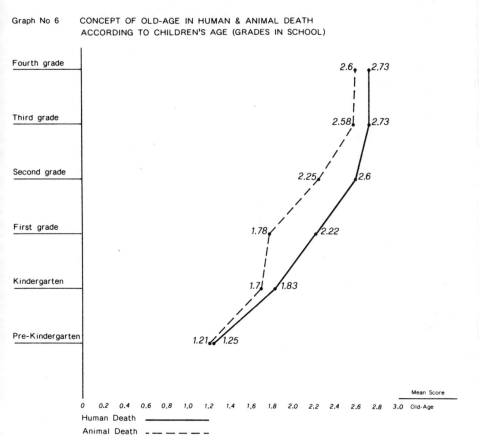

Graph No 6   CONCEPT OF OLD-AGE IN HUMAN & ANIMAL DEATH
ACCORDING TO CHILDREN'S AGE (GRADES IN SCHOOL)

Fourth grade   2.6   2.73

Third grade   2.58   2.73

Second grade   2.25   2.6

First grade   1.78   2.22

Kindergarten   1.7   1.83

Pre-Kindergarten   1.21 1.25

Mean Score

0   0.2   0.4   0.6   0.8   1.0   1.2   1.4   1.6   1.8   2.0   2.2   2.4   2.6   2.8   3.0   Old-Age

Human Death ───────────

Animal Death ─ ─ ─ ─ ─ ─

7. Short Description of Study: How Orphanhood Affects the Conceptualization of Death

In view of the great importance that the conceptualization of death has for the adjustment and rehabilitation of orphans, we wanted to test and learn whether the fact of becoming an orphan makes it possible for the child, or even makes it easier for him/her to develop concepts of death. Or perhaps, it delays the development of death concepts, compared with children who are not orphans. It has been found that experience is an important condition for the development of various physical concepts (Flavell, 1977), but does this assumption hold for the development of traumatic concepts related to a parent's death?

In order to answer these questions, 948 children between the ages of 4-12 were tested: 476 were orphans and 472 non-orphans served as control group. The control group was pair-matched with the orphan group in terms of the following four background variables: sex, age of child, parents' country of origin, mother's and father's education.

The research population (948 children) was tested individually by means of the "Questionnaire for Examination of Human and Animal Death Conceptualization of Children"*, and by means of two verbal sub-tests of the Wechsler Intelligence Scale for Children (Wechsler 1974): "General Information" and "Similarities" sub-tests. The first sub-test evaluates the child's absorption ability, his manner of organizing and utilizing information, the second sub-test evaluates the level of the child's verbal conceptualization and abstraction. The two areas evaluated by these sub-tests, are directly related to the child's intellectual ability to conceptualize death. Each child was given a point score for both sub-tests, which reflects his level of intelligence. Among many other statistical analyses, the two groups were compared by means of the 't' test for comparing means.

---

* See detailed description and its psychometric characteristics on page 195.

Conceptualization	Group of children	Average Score	Standard Deviation	N	t
Death of Humans	Orphans	12.0	2.9	476	1.89*
	Non-orphans	12.3	2.4	472	
Death of Animals	Orphans	10.8	3.0	476	
	Non-orphans	10.9	2.9	472	.35
Total Concept of Death	Orphans	22.6	5.0	476	1.94*
	Non-orphans	23.5	4.7	472	

* significant p 0.05

The table shows that the non-orphans (control group) scored significantly higher than the orphans, both in the total conceptualization of death and in conceptualization of the death of humans. While there was no difference between the two groups in conceptualization of the death of animals.

These results can be explained in a number of ways: since the two groups were similar in I.Q., age, sex and parents' education, except orphanhood, it can be assumed that the emotions connected with their loss prevented the orphans from reaching the level of death conceptualization reached by non-orphans. This assumption is supported by the fact that the difference occurs in the conceptualization of the death of humans and not that of animals.

An additional explanation of the difference between the two groups may lie in the different ways families have in dealing with death. Perhaps the adults in families in mourning do not help the children conceptualize death, and in this way delay the development of concepts of death in the orphans. The experience of death of the parent does not in itself make it possible for the child to develop the concepts on his own. To achieve this the child must be helped by the adults. In other words, experiencing death of a parent aids orphans in death conceptualization, only if adults in their environment intervene and help them*.

*   For additional parts of 'this study see: 1) Smilansky, S. "Different Mourning Patterns and the Orphan's Intellectual Ability to understand Concepts of Death", *Advances in Thanatology*, vol. 5, No. 2 N.Y. Arno Press, 1981. 2) Smilansky, S. "Learning, Social and Emotional Adjustment of Elementary School Orphans", in Spielberger, C.D., Sarason, I.G. and Milgram, N. (Eds.) *"Stress and Anxiety"*, vol. 8, Hemisphere Pub. Co., 1981.

8. Short Description of the Study: "Use of Poems as a Means to Help Young Children Understand and Cope with Death" (1982)

15 Poems describing children's encounter with death, are included in the book. They were written by the author and tested in Israel in an experimental study, of which a short description follows:

The study included 288 children, aged 5-12, who were confronted during the last year with death, either in school, or community or in the family. 73 % (210 children) of these children either came on their own to the adults working in pre-school and school (teachers, remedial teachers, counsellors, social workers, psychologists, etc.) and initiated talks related to death. Or, when adults working in school initiated (individually or in groups) talks and encouraged the children to speak, sooner or later these children asked questions, expressed their doubts, worries and feelings related to death.

27 % (78 children of same ages and similar socio-economic background) of children refused to communicate with their teachers, remedial teachers, counsellors or psychologists, and share their information, doubts, questions and feelings, related to their confrontation with death. Of these, 40 children were included in the study.

The 40 children were divided randomly into two groups: 20 children in the experimental group and 20 children in the control group. The children in each group met individually and in groups with counsellors during 16 one-hour sessions, two sessions a week.

In the experimental group the counsellors used these poems. At the beginning of each of the 16 sessions (sometimes during the whole session) the children read the poems and talked about the child and situation described in the poem. If during a session a certain child on his own has chosen to talk about himself, or compare himself or his problems, to those described in the poem, he/she could do that. But during the first 5 sessions the counsellors never suggested or encouraged a child to tell about himself. From the 6th until the 16th session, although always at the beginning of each session a poem was read and discussed, the counsellors gradually encouraged the children to compare themselves with the child or situation described in the poem. For example: "What would you suggest the boy/girl in the poem to do"; or "Was your situation similar to her/his? or "Did you have similar or different feelings? What are they?" etc.

In the control group, during the 16 sessions the counsellors made various attempts (individually and in groups) to talk to the children and to encourage them directly to talk about their encounters with death, without using any written material or telling any stories.

After 16 sessions the results of the study showed that as compared with the control group, a significantly larger number of children in the experimental group opened – up and talked about their encounter with death: They asked questions, described their understanding of death and expressed feelings (fear, anger, pain, guilt, etc.). There was also some change in the control group, but limited and the difference between the two groups was highly significant.

List of poems included in the book